Women

who
love
books
too much

Women

who
love
books
too much

Bibliophiles,
Bluestockings &
Prolific Pens

Brenda Knight

BARNES & NOBLE BOOKS
NEW YORK

Published by MJF Books
Fine Communications
322 Eighth Avenue
New York, NY 10001

Women Who Love Books Too Much
LC Control Number 2004101090
ISBN 1-56731-660-3

Portions of this book have appeared in *Hell's Belles* by Seale Ballenger and *Sheroes* by Varla Ventura. Reprinted by permission of Conari Press.

This edition published by arrangement with Conari Press, an imprint of Red Wheel/Weiser LLC.

Manufactured in the United States of America on acid-free paper ∞

MJF Books and the MJF colophon are trademarks of Fine Creative Media, Inc.

VB   10   9   8   7   6   5   4   3   2   1

This is for

Mrs. Evelyn Gammon

my late and great teacher who taught me to read in the first grade and made me believe in myself. I'll never forget the support and encouragement she gave me to pursue my dreams. I also dedicate this to every teacher, librarian, and volunteer who instills a love of books in their students.

Women *who love* books *too much*

foreword *by Vicki León*

author of the *Uppity Women* series

With her new book, Brenda Knight has made it not only legitimate but cool to be book-mad. As a woman with a chronic case of bibliomania, I'm delighted to see we're out of the closet. Of course, it makes me anxious, too: will there be enough books for everybody, if, you know, all those other people become bibliophiles?

As a student of history, I've learned that we're in supremely good company. Ever since there have been books, there have been bookworms. That's more than 4,000 years of voracious reading—and a lot of it accomplished by women. The making of books was a scary new technology: marks made on clay or silk or paper became time capsules of knowledge. They conveyed secrets. They ignored distances. No wonder that, early on, books became sacrosanct in ways we cannot even imagine.

From earliest times, females horned in on the reading, transcribing, and authoring of books. Take ancient Mesopotamia, for instance. Although it made males quite testy, women occasionally became scribes. In fact, the earliest author we know of in history—male or female—was a priestess and poet named Enheduanna of Ur, whose work dates from 2500 B.C.E. Only boys were supposed to learn reading and writing; so many women managed to do so, however, that a distinctively female written dialect called *emesal* came into being.

Books in Mesopotamia were palm-sized or smaller, durable and portable. They were made of clay and able to be reused. They sound suspiciously like the Palmpilots and e-books of today, don't they?

With literacy came cupidity. Thousands of years ago, women lusted for books. And began to collect them. One of the earliest bibliophiles was—surprise—the world's most famous sex goddess and political schemer: Cleopatra the Seventh. At Alexandria, the Egyptian queen possessed a world library that was without parallel. A lifelong student of philosophy, she got a voluptuous enjoyment from reading. When Marc Anthony set out to win Cleopatra's heart, he knew just what to give her: the library at Pergamum in Asia Minor—the second most wondrous in the world. (It was, however, a nightmare to gift wrap.)

A few hundred years later, highly educated Roman women took part in one of Christianity's great literacy projects. Women like Paula and her daughter Eustochium spent thirty-five years translating the Bible into Greek and Latin, under the direction of early Christian writer and glory-hound Jerome, who took all subsequent credit for the work of his corps of skilled female readers and translators.

On the other side of the globe, Asian women had been hip-deep in bibliomania since the eighth century, when a bright Japanese empress named Koken ordered up a 1 million print run of religious verse—Asia's first block printing project.

From the eleventh through thirteenth centuries, a golden age of reading and writing, with women at its forefront, bloomed among Japanese literati. The hands-down superstar of the age was Murasaki Shikibu, whose psychological fiction, *The Tale of Genji,* is now considered the world's first "modern" novel. As in Mesopotamia, the number of women involved in reading and writing reached such a critical mass that the phonetic Japanese writing system, called *hiragana,* came to be called "woman's hand."

In medieval times, nuns fought to save the collected wisdom of the world in permanent form. Although literacy took a nosedive among Europeans, here and there women still managed to read, write, and collect books. Eleanor of Aquitaine, for instance, and Heloise, the nun whose hots for Abelard overshadowed her love of books. There were lesser lights we haven't heard much about, too, like Mahaut, the French Countess of Artois. Glamorous Mahaut traveled with sixty horses, forty servants, and her best illuminated books carried in special leather bags. One of her favorites was *The Book of the Great Cham*—the tell-all by Marco Polo.

So go on, do some guilt-free indulging in the pages of Brenda Knight's basket of literary bonbons. She has gathered a wealth of delectable stories in which to immerse ourselves, a bite at a time. Let's hear it for bibliophiles and book ladies—our richest yet most non-fattening vice. Thanks to women from Aphra Behn to Zelda Fitzgerald, we can enter the most magical looking glass of all: the bright world beyond the moment, the one we call "literacy."

Women
who
love
books
too much

Introduction

Women Who Love Books Too Much

Chances are, if you're reading this, you ARE one! A woman who loves books too much (WWLBTM), that is—a special breed suffering from a singular syndrome with certain telltale symptoms: Does your heart race when you see a new book by one of your favorite authors? Do you feel a little dizzy when you walk into a bookstore packed with hundreds of new books? Are you overcome when you receive your monthly book club mailer? Do you lose a little sleep the night before your reading group meets? Have you called in sick because you needed to stay home and read? Are you happiest when deep in the pages of or deep in discussion about the complexities of a book? Do you read the book review section of the newspaper before you read your horoscope?

I thought so. You've got it. And bad.

Well, you're not alone. There are others. I'm sure you know a few—certainly the harried bookseller down your street, the one who seems to be there no matter when you stop in, whether it's nine in the morning or nine at night. The women in your book group, too, are part of the sisterhood, as is the shy girl in the corner café, nose buried in a book, never looking up. And my sister, Martha Reed, a teacher who goes on vacations to—oh, how decadent!—do nothing but read.

My sister and the rest of us WWLBTM are bibliophiles or bibliolists, the proper names for book lovers. If you have a collection of books that is threatening to take over house and home, chances are you are suffering from bibliomania, "an exaggerated liking for acquiring books," says my dictionary. And if you've come by those books dishonestly, you have bibliokleptomania, a penchant for pinching rather than paying.

You know what? We modern women don't have it so bad. At least now, a bookish woman is perceived as fairly innocuous. Only a hundred years ago, a "bluestocking" was thought of as dangerous, possibly insurrectionist, and, any way you cut it, trouble. Can you imagine not being taught to read? Can you picture not being allowed to write? Well, not so long ago, that was exactly the case. As you will soon discover, women of colonial America might be ostracized for having the audacity to form a book discussion group, about the Bible, no less! And visionary women authors were often seen as madwomen.

Here, gathered together for the first time, are the stories of those women whose love of books compelled them to put their lives on the line. These are the women who made it possible for us modern WWLBTM to freely read, write, and discuss the tomes we so treasure.

Without the initial efforts of our foremothers, women wouldn't be at helms of multinational publishing houses, receive million dollar advances, or write Pulitzer Prize-winning novels.

This book is intended to be a travel guide from the library to the Left Bank of Paris and back again. Moreover, it is a tribute to those solitary nuns who scratched out their feminist theologies in anchorite cells, to slave girls who composed classical poetry the equal (at least) of that written by contemporary men, to the biblical "J," to Saint Jerome's nameless army who wrote and translated the Bible we know today. It's a gift of gratitude to the defiant dames who survived rejection letters, bad reviews, and jail time, a big bouquet to the first novelists, pioneer poets, and innovative intellectuals who hosted salons. From the mass-marketed darlings of the mystery world and the romance writers who steal our hearts to the bravehearted who find themselves banned and blacklisted into obscurity, this collection of profiles offers a look at the price women have had to pay to be creative, to be political, and to break new ground. Their surviving, and in some cases ongoing, work continues to affect people worldwide. A great book or poem is, at its zenith, an expression of the divine. For you, for me, for the women portrayed here, to read and to write is to live!

one

First Ladies of Literature

Mothers of Invention

HATS AND PEN CAPS OFF to these pioneers who paved the way for every woman who followed in their courageous footsteps. Here are stories of their struggles, unmitigated moxie, and abject determination to express themselves and share their views with readers. No fainthearts, these women survived jailing, name-calling, and cruelest of all, having their reputations and accomplishments hidden for decades and even centuries. In addition to the women profiled here, let's also salute Lady Murasaki Shikubu, the first novelist of any gender, whose novel, *The Tale of Genji*, depicted court life, love, and adventure in eleventh-century Japan.

7

The literary laureates are rousing as well, slowly but surely knocking down barriers and opening minds in their wake (and in this category, let us not forget to acknowledge brilliant Marguerite Yourcenar, the first woman "immortal," who in 1980 was elected to the French Academy by secret ballot over the memorable objections of one member who claimed, "The Academie has survived over 300 years without women and it could survive another 300 without them.") Aphra Behn, Charles II's spy, dared to write for a living and expected to be paid for it. (She also went unacknowledged for 300 years as a precursor to the novel.) From Saint Jerome's unaccredited nuns who really "wrote" the Bible to poet-slave Phillis Wheatley, these first ladies of literature deserve credit for showing us that real inspiration can come only from being true to yourself at any cost.

§ ENHEDUANNA *sacred poet of Sumeria*

Any discussion of breakthrough writers must surely begin with Enheduanna, the first recorded writer of either gender. Born into the royal family of Sumeria, in the area that in the modern world is known as southern Iraq, she served as high priestess to the moon god and goddess, Nanna and Inanna. Her poem-hymns were written in cuneiform on clay tablets, and they escaped the fate of many other documents of the time, disintegrating into forgotten dust. Her portrait, carved on a limestone disk, was discovered in an excavation of the ancient city of Ur.

THE MUSES *the nine Greek goddesses of arts who "inspire" artists*

Calliope, the "Fair Voiced," is the eldest of Muses and presides over epic poetry.

Clio, the "Proclaimer" and the muse of history, carries a scroll of knowledge.

Erato, the "Lovely" with her lyre, rules over love poetry and mimicry.

Euterpe, the "Giver of Pleasure," plays a flute. Her domain is music.

Melpomene, the "Songstress," wears the mask of tragedy, over which she presides.

Polyhymnia, is "she of many hymns." Wearing a veil, she is the muse of sacred poetry.

Terpischore, "the Whirler," has the domain of dance.

Thalia, "the Flourishing," wears the mask of comedy and is the muse for both comedy and idyllic poetry.

Urania, "the Heavenly," is the astronomer's muse who wears a crown of stars and foretells the future through astrology.

The Three Fates determine all our destinies: *Clotho* spins the thread of life, *Lachesis* chooses the length and outcome, and *Atropos* cuts the thread of life.

Her greatest work is the "Hymn to Inanna"; it is difficult to know whether she employs poetic license when she describes being sent into exile during a time of political upheaval. Readers can't help but notice that the poem "Nin-me-sar-ra" describes how Enheduanna's prayers to the moon god Nanna went unanswered and how Nanna's daughter, the moon goddess Inanna, came to her aid, exacting justice and restoring her to her rightful place as priestess. More than 4,000 years old, the poem is simple, powerful, and beautiful.

> *Let it be known! That this is not said of Nanna, It is said of you—his is your greatness. You alone are the High one.*

Enheduanna

───────

§ MARGERY KEMPE *medieval autobiographer*

Margery Kempe herself is the best source of information on her life, having written her autobiography—the first of its kind in English—in the fourteenth century. Born in 1373, she was the daughter of the mayor of Lynn, Norfolk, England. She married late for the times—at twenty—and got pregnant right away. Undergoing a wretchedly long and painful labor, she went mad and became violent, tearing at her flesh, screaming, having visions of devils, and screaming obscenities about her husband, her neighbors and friends, and herself. She claimed to be calmed when Christ himself appeared to her in a vision, and indeed she returned to her life as a wife and mother and bore thirteen more children.

Margery Kempe was profoundly changed, however, by her vision and decided to dedicate her life to Christian mysticism, continuing to experience visitations and fits of weeping. She undertook a journey to the Holy Land, traveling alone from England across the continent to the Middle East. Her religious intentions meant nothing to those she met along the way; she was treated horribly, called a whore and a heretic, and was jailed for her efforts, forced to defend herself with no help. Her recollections of the time depict a woman heeding a calling, torn between her love of Christ and her love of family.

Despite all her tribulations, she managed to live a long life. Unable to write herself, she worked with hesitant scribes to compose her life story. Called *The Book of Margery Kempe,* this literary treasure was lost for nearly 500 years. Thankfully, a copy was rediscovered in 1934, and Britain's first autobiographical text is again telling the story of the extraordinary, ordinary housewife and mother.

> *And sometimes those that men think were revelations, are deceits and illusions, and therefore it is not expedient to give readily credence to every stirring.*
>
> Margery Kempe

§ APHRA BEHN *living by the pen*

It is amazing that the name of Aphra Behn, England's first professional woman writer, is not better known. While a handful of her contemporaries—Anne Finch, the Countess of Winchilea, and

Margaret Cavendish, the Duchess of Newcastle—wrote for the entertainment of a small circle of friends, Aphra Behn was paid for her work and undertook it as her profession. Her circumstances were far different from such courtly ladies, as well. She was a widow of modest means and used her talent to survive.

Behn's parentage is unclear. We know she was born in 1640 and traveled with her foster family to Surinam in the West Indies. Some biographers say she was involved in a slave rebellion in 1663. This same year, she and her family and fellow travelers were the first Europeans to visit a tribe of Indians in the West Indies. The following year, she returned to England and married a London merchant, Behn, who died of the plague in 1665.

After the tragedy of her short-lived marriage, Aphra Behn needed an income and was fortunate to have an opportunity to enter King Charles II's private force of spies. "Such public toils of state affairs unusual with my sex or in my years," she admitted. Behn was sent to Antwerp, where she proved to be a most able spy, but she did not receive her promised payment and was sent to a London debtor's prison in 1668. While in jail, she determined never to subject herself to anyone's mercy again and vowed to make her way independently and by her own wits.

APHRA BEHN *the first female professional writer in the English language*

She wrote her first play and saw it published partly because of the sheer novelty that she was a woman. The play, *The Forced Marriage,* was staged in London in 1670. From then on, Behn's progress was rapid. Her career as a professional playwright established, she wrote and published fourteen plays, encompassing many styles from farce to drama, including *The Rover, Sir Patient Fancy, The City Heiress,* and *The Roundheads.* She also began publishing poetry and comic verse. Always skirting the edge of controversy, she wrote some very sensual poems, which shocked the readers of the day, prompting Anne Finch to comment, "a little too loosely she writ." Criticism of her work fell consistently in one of two extremes of wild praise or scorching criticism, often focusing on her femaleness: the "body of a Venus and the mind of a Minerva," the "English Sappho," or, cruelly, "that lewd harlot."

Behn's response was to carry on, pointing out that the great male writers of the day suffered no public shame at their openly erotic references. When the London theater fell on hard times after the glories of the Restoration, Behn turned her hand to writing prose fiction: *Love Letters between a Nobleman and His Sister,* published in 1684, followed by *The Fair, Jilt, Agnes de Castro,* and her opus, *Oroonoko.* Written in 1688, *Oroonoko* was loosely autobiographical, retelling a fictionalized version of her journey to Surinam as a young woman and her protest against slavery. This account is widely regarded as the first novel in English literature.

Sadly, a mere year after her triumph, she passed away, ill and impoverished. She continued to suffer denigration after her death by many who disapproved of her fiercely independent spirit. But Behn blazed the trail for every woman writer to come after her. Three hundred years later, Virginia Woolf penned this homage: "All women together ought to let flowers fall upon the tomb of Aphra Behn, for it was she who earned them the right to speak their minds."

I'll only say as I have touched before, that plays have no great room for that which is men's great advantage over women.

Aphra Behn

LADY MARY CHUDLEIGH

A contemporary of Aphra Behn, Lady Mary Chudleigh wrote a verse response to British minister John Sprint, who in 1700 wrote *The Bride-Women's Counselor*, which instructed women to love, honor, and obey in no uncertain terms. Chudleigh wrote, in verse, a series including *The Female Advocate; or A Plea for Just Liberty of the Tender Sex* and notably *Married Women and the Ladies Defense; or the Bride-Woman's Counselor Answered*. John Sprint was indeed resoundingly answered with Chudleigh's beautifully wrought feminist rhetoric scorning the tacit rules that kept women "Debarred from knowledge, banished from the schools, And with the utmost industry bred fools," entrapped in the "mean, low trivial cares of life." She exhorted women to "read and think, and think and read again." Sadly, we know very little of her life except that she married Sir George Chudleigh and lost her children at very young ages. Her poems were crafted skillfully and with a keen intelligence and courageous idealism. Writing in 1700 and 1701, Lady Mary was well ahead of her time.

Wife and servant are the same,
But only differ in the name

—Lady Mary Chudleigh, *To the Ladies*

§ CHRISTINE DE PISAN

the first woman writer to be published in English

In the same way that, according to Virginia Woolf, English women writers are indebted to Aphra Behn, Italian women writers, including Nobel laureate Grazia Deledda, are indebted to Christine de Pisan. Three hundred years before Aphra Behn set pen to paper, de Pisan was earning her way as a writer.

Born in 1364, she was the daughter of a scientist and scholar, Thomas de Pisan, a Venetian court-appointed astrologer to the French king Charles V. Her girlhood saw a rare advantage for Christine: a classical education. She loved France and claimed it as her heart's home. Her father saw to it that she was educated as well as any man, and Christine learned French, Latin, arithmetic, and geometry. She married Etienne du Castel, who was nine years her senior, at fifteen. In three short years they had three children, and du Castel died around the time of the third baby's birth. At barely nineteen, Christine de Pisan was left to support her children and several hapless relatives, and did so with her talent for prose and poetry.

She claimed to write constantly, noting "in the short space of six years, between 1397 and 1403. . . fifteen important books, without mentioning minor essays, which, compiled, make seventy large copy-books." Among her books are a biography of Charles V, Philip of Burgundy, and *Le Livre de Paix*. In the latter, an instruction on rearing princes and a rebuttal to the bestselling "bible of courtly love," *The Romance of the Rose,* de Pisan she seeks to repair a woman's reputation that had been ruined by the popular epic poem.

After a writing career that lasted twenty-nine years, Christine retired to a convent. In 1429, just before her death, she wrote a book honoring Joan of Arc. It was, writes Vicki León in *Uppity Women of Medival Times,* "the only French book ever written about the Maid of Orleans in her lifetime."

While she was alive, Christine de Pisan received unstintingly positive reviews for her work and was compared favorably to Cicero and Cato. Her work stands the test of time. In 1521 *Le Livre du duc des vrais aman* was published in England as *The Book of the Duke of True Lovers,* the first book published in English by a woman. Her *City of Women* has been rediscovered in the twentieth century and is taught in literature courses worldwide.

§ ANNE BRADSTREET *Pilgrim's Progress*

Fifty years before Aphra Behn shocked English society, Anne Bradstreet wrote the first book of poetry published in the American colonies. Arriving with her family in 1630, Anne Bradstreet saw the raw new America as opportunity to create a new way of being: "I found a new world and new manners, at which my heart rose," she wrote.

She was at once a pioneer and a typically religious member of her Puritan community. She had come from a privileged background, afforded her by her father Thomas Dudley, who ran the estate of an earl of Lincoln. Anne Bradstreet was allowed to visit the earl's library freely and she took full advantage, reading exhaustively religious texts, poetry, and classics.

In 1628, she married Simon Bradstreet, a graduate of Cambridge who worked as a steward for the earl. Anne's husband was nine years older than she and equally educated. Life on the earl's estate was filled with ease, comfort, and security, but that soon changed.

The devout religiosity of the Dudleys led them to believe they should prove their devotion to God though trials and tribulations. These they found in plentitude in the New World. The whole family moved lock, stock, and barrel to the Massachusetts colony, where Anne's father and husband both served as governors. They suffered from the cold, malaria, starvation, and the harsh, unforgiving climate of this savage new world.

Part of the Puritan ethos included stringent second-class status for all women, for it was God's will that a woman should be subordinate, a constant helpmate to man, and humble, with no personal ambitions. In these circumstances, writing was dangerous. In 1645, Massachusetts governor John Winthrop lamented the sad straying of "a godly young woman" who was mentally unstable and in a weakened, fallen state, gave "herself wholly to reading and writing, and [had] written many books." He had banished Anne Hutchinson seven years earlier for daring to interpret religious doctrine in her own way.

Anne Bradstreet's brother-in-law John Woodbridge didn't hold to the belief that women couldn't have their own intellectual lives. He had Anne Bradstreet's poetry, collected in *The Tenth Muse,* printed in London, where it proved to be highly "vendable," according to London booksellers. Woodbridge provided a foreword to the book, making clear that it was "the work of a woman, honoured and esteemed where she lives, for. . . the exact diligence in her place, and discreet managing of her family occasions, and these poems are but the fruit of some few hours, curtailed from her sleep and other refreshments."

A devoted mother, Anne Bradstreet gave birth to eight children and, as "helpmate," saw her husband rise to considerable prosperity and power in the colony. With little time to rest or write, her literary output ceased. She suffered from continuing symptoms of the smallpox she had contracted as a child and died in 1673.

Though she was forgotten for centuries, twentieth-century poets, particularly Conrad Aiken and John Berryman, have recognized her contribution in various tributes. Adrienne Rich demands her genius be honored: "To have written. . . the first good poems in America, while rearing eight children lying frequently sick, keeping house at the edge of the wilderness, was to have managed a poet's range and extension within confines as severe as any American poet has confronted."

> *Fool. I do grudge the Muses did not part*
> *Twixt him and me that overfluent store. . . .*

From the Prologue, *Anne Bradstreet*

---

§ MARY MANLEY *the first bestselling woman author*

It is amazing that Mary Manley is not better known; she was the first British woman to have a career as a political journalist, the first female author of a bestseller, and the very first woman to be jailed for her writing. Born in 1663, she was ahead of her time in her advocacy for women's rights and her willingness to take risks with her own comfortable life to fight for these rights. Manley decried the inequity that saw women punished for acts any man could do freely. Her greatest passion was that women should as writers have equal opportunity with men.

She herself was prolific, authoring short stories, plays, satires, political essays, and letters. She replaced Jonathan Swift of *Gulliver's*

Travels fame as the editor of the Tory paper, the *Examiner,* yet she remains relatively unknown while he has a permanent place in the canon, widely read and widely taught. Swift's achievements seem Lilliputian in comparison to Mary Manley's feat.

Her bestselling satire, *Secret Memoirs and Manners of Several Persons of Quality of Both Sexes from the New Atlantis, an Island in the Mediterranean,* was aimed at the Tory opposition, the Whigs. The poison prose swiftly hit target. Manley and her publishers were thrown in jail, and the adage about any kind of publicity—even bad publicity—being good held true. Readers bought the book in droves to figure out who the real people were behind the thinly veiled biographical sketches. Clever lass, Manley's absolutely public *Secret Memoirs* included much to titillate and tantalize, including Corinna, the maiden who staunchly refuses to get married, and a mysterious lesbian group called the Cabal.

As a challenge at the height of her fame, Mary Manley described herself as "a ruined woman," and in a fictionalized autobiography revealed her betrayal and entrapment into marriage to a cousin who took her money and ran. Inspired by her father, a writer who held a high office, Mary wasn't ruined at all, but a huge success as a writer who chose lovers of standing as peers and lived life on her own terms. Before there was Rebecca, Danielle, and Jackie, there was Mary! This seventeenth-century virago paved the way for Joe Klein's bestselling political satire, *Primary Colors,* and every female who ever mounted the bestseller list.

> *She who has all the muses in her head, wanted to be caressed in a poetical manner.*
>
> Mary Manley from *Secret Memoirs*

§ LUCY TERRY PRINCE *pioneer and poet*

As one of the first black American poets, Lucy Terry has yet to receive her due. She was born in 1730 in Africa. Kidnapped as a baby, she was brought to the colony of Rhode Island and was purchased at the age of five by Ensign Ebenezer Wells of Deerfield, Massachusetts, to be a servant. Wells had Lucy baptized on June 15, 1735, at the insistence of his mistress, during the "Great Awakening," an effort to uproot Calvinism in New England. As many blacks as possible were baptized in this mass conversion effort.

Little is known of her life until age sixteen, when she was inspired to poetry by the bloody massacre of two colonial families by sixty Indians in "the Bars"—a colonial word for "meadow"—an area outside Deerfield. George Sheldon, a Deerfield historian, declares Lucy's ballad, "The Bars Fight," to be "the first rhymed narration of an American slave" and believes it was recited and sung by Lucy. He further describes it as "the fullest contemporary account of that bloody tragedy which has been preserved." While the original document has been lost, it was passed down in the oral tradition and printed for the first time by Josiah Gilbert Holland in 1855.

Lucy went on to marry Abijah Prince, a slave more than twice her age. He was a landowner and one of the chartered founders of Sunderland in the state of Vermont; he bought his wife's freedom. They had a happy marriage, and Lucy loved to entertain and tell stories to their guests.

In 1760, they moved to Guilford, Vermont, after Abijah Prince inherited a hundred-acre plot of land. They received threats from white neighbors, which Lucy publicly protested, demanding protection from the governor's council. She and Abijah had six children and wanted college educations to be available to them. Once again, Lucy protested discrimination against blacks, this time in the ranks of higher education, orating for three hours. She was not successful in this case, but gained a national reputation for her verbal skills, going so far as to plead in the Supreme Court her own case against a land-grabbing neighbor. Historians hold that presiding Justice Samuel Chase stated that Lucy's discourse was superior to that of any Vermont lawyer in the court. She outlived Abijah, who passed away in 1794, and returned to Sunderland to live. When she died at the age of ninety-one, she left behind a legacy of freedom fighting for women and black people alike.

§ PHILLIS WHEATLEY *the muse of Africa*

While Lucy Terry Prince remains fairly obscure, Phillis Wheatley has been acknowledged for her role as one of the earliest women writers in America. She is, in fact, generally regarded as the first black woman writer, and, after Anne Bradstreet, the second woman writer in America. A poet, her verse expresses guarded pride about her "sable race" and subtle treatment of the subject of slavery, though her letters express her strong feelings about it. She called herself "Africa's Muse" in her "Hymn to Humanity."

She and Lucy's stories begin the same way: Phillis was kidnapped by slave traders as a child in Africa and, along with as many as eighty other young girls, shipped from Senegal, brought to the port of Boston, and sold into slavery in 1761.

Phillis' fortunes were a bit better than others were, in that she was purchased by a kindhearted Christian woman, Susannah Wheatley, who took pity on the forlorn child wrapped in a dirty scrap of carpeting. Phillis' price was a bargain; the Wheatleys, guessing her to be around seven years old because of missing front teeth, took her into their home on King Street and gave her their last name, as was the practice with slaves.

The Wheatleys noticed how curious and alert Phillis was and judged her to be of exceptional intelligence. When she tried to write on the wall, their teenaged daughter Mary Wheatley started to teach Phillis in earnest. At the end of a year's time, Phillis was reading and writing with ease and had also learned, according to her master's recollection, a "little astronomy, some ancient and modern geography, a little ancient history, a fair knowledge of the Bible, and a thoroughly appreciative acquaintance with the most important Latin classics, especially the works of Virgil and Ovid." Phillis became, in his words again, "one of the most highly educated young women in Boston," and went on to study and translate Latin. Indeed one of her interpretations of a Latin tale by Ovid was published.

She also liked to compose verse and loved the brilliantly crafted poetry of Alexander Pope, whom she took as her model. In 1767, fourteen-year-old Phillis wrote the first of many occasional poems, "To the University of Cambridge," thirty-two blank verses of counsel for college boys. The Wheatleys proved to be generous to the girl and encouraged her to pursue her poetics, providing her with paper and pen in case of a sudden inspiration. Phillis had a delicate constitution and was only allowed to perform light chores such as dusting and polishing.

One of her occasional poems, "On the Death of the Reverend Mr. George Whitefield," brought her to the eyes of the world when it appeared on a broadside, printed in Boston in 1770, that was reprinted throughout the colonies and in England. Her story was sensationalized as the work of "a servant girl. . . but nine years in this country from Africa." She was ushered into literary and social circles she would normally have been forbidden to enter, though, because of her slave status, she was not allowed to dine at her hosts' tables.

In 1772, Phillis considered the prospects of collecting her poems into a volume, and the ever-supportive John Wheatley sent a manuscript and a letter of introduction and biographical information to Archibald Bell in London. Bell and the Countess of Huntington, to whom he had shown Phillis' poems, doubted that an African girl had really written the work and required the testament of no less than eighteen prominent Bostonians.

Meanwhile, Phillis' health weakened and the Wheatley's reasoned a trip abroad might bolster her. Accompanied by Nathaniel Wheatley, Mary's twin, on a business trip, Phillis set out to London and was an immediate cause célèbre, thanks to an introduction into society provide by the Countess of Huntington. She was feted and flattered in a land free from slavery. According to one account, "Thoughtful people praised her; titled people dined her, and the press extolled the name of Phillis Wheatley, the African poetess." Her single published book,

PHILLIS WHEATLEY *This Senegalese captive was sold into slavery in 1761 and began composing poems in English a year later.*

Poems on Various Subjects, Religious and Moral, was published in 1773 and was dedicated to none other than the countess. Complete with a portrait of Phillis holding a quill pen drawn by Scipio Moorhead, slave artist and poet, it contained thirty-nine poems.

The following year, Susannah Wheatley, the only mother figure Phillis had known in the land of her captors, died. With the Revolutionary War impending, Phillis wrote a letter to General George Washington, who was impressed by the "elegant lines" of her missive and invited her to be received by him and his officers. When John Wheatley passed away, Phillis was set free.

She married a Boston grocer a month later, a handsome free black man who claimed to have worked as a lawyer and physician as well as merchant. His looks and talent are said to have led to a degree of "arrogance" and "disdain" for work, which allegedly saw the newlyweds into poverty. Two of their three children died, and Phillis labored at a cheap boarding house to support herself and her remaining child. At thirty-one, she died, followed almost immediately by her child. They were buried together in a location that remains unknown. The last attention the "African poetess" received for her writing talent was a poem she wrote about the death of her baby son, published in 1784 in *Boston* magazine. This was one of several compositions from the last part of her life, all set to be published in honor of Benjamin Franklin, to whom she had dedicated the book. The manuscript disappeared along with all trace of Phillis Wheatley's work as a mature poet.

> *Imagination! Who can sing thy force? Or who describe the swiftness of thy course?*

Phillis Wheatley

§ HARRIET E. ADAMS WILSON *provocateur*

Like many other literary women, Harriet Wilson was also left out of history books. She was the first black woman to publish a novel in English and the first black person, male or female, to publish a novel in America.

Sadly, we know precious little about this author. Harriet E. Adams Wilson is believed to have been born in Fredericksburg, Virginia, in 1807 or 1808, trained in millinery as her trade, and was deserted and left in poverty by her sailor husband who impregnated her before the abandonment. Her son from this relationship, George Mason Wilson, died at age seven, a year after the publication of the one novel it is known that Wilson wrote.

Her groundbreaking work, *Our Nig,* a title deliberately chosen for its challenge and daring, was printed by George C. Rand and Avery of Boston. It is believed Wilson self-published *Our Nig* to prove a political point, as evidenced by the full title, *Our Nig, or, Sketches from the Life of a Free Black, in A Two-Story White House, North, Showing That Slavery's Shadows Fall Even There* by "Our Nig."

Our Nig was ignored by reviewers and readers and barely sold. Wilson's work was in the dustbin of lost history until Henry Louis Gates, Jr., discovered it and reissued it in 1983. Gates observes that the provocative title probably contributed to the novel's near oblivion. The plot, a marriage between a white woman and a black man, would have alienated many readers.

> *Example rendered her words efficacious. Day by day there was a manifest change of deportment towards "Nig."*

Harriet E. Adams Wilson

25

Poet Sara Teasdale, known now for the evocative intensity of her language, was brought up in the truest Victorian tradition in the late 1880s in St. Louis, Missouri. She was pampered and protected, but, like a hothouse flower starved for light, felt smothered by her parents' watchful restrictions. Imaginative and sensitive, Sara found her only solace in writing. In 1907, when she was twenty-three, *Reedy's Mirror,* a St. Louis weekly paper, published her work for the first time.

By twenty-six, she was desperate to break free of the hampering bonds of dependency on her parents. The only way she could manage this was to marry. She didn't find the prospects particularly appealing, but it seemed preferable to her stifling life at home. Her hopes included a serious writing career, which she found incompatible with the role of wife and mother. When she discovered she was pregnant, she had an abortion and obtained a divorce, hoping for the independence she believed would foster her writing. This unfortunate series of events sent her into a depression and failing health. From that point on, she lived the secluded life of a semi-invalid.

Teasdale's beautiful poetry bespeaking the secrets of the human heart created an international reputation, beginning with her early *Love Songs.* Subsequently, she channeled her painful struggles for freedom from oppressive Victorian mores in *Flame and Shadow.* She won the prestigious Columbia University Poetry Society prize, and in 1917 won the Pulitzer Prize for Poetry for *Love Songs,* earning her place in history as the first poet to receive this prestigious award. Ultimately, the delicate despair described in her poems won out, and Sara Teasdale committed suicide in 1933.

O, beauty, are you not enough?
Why am I crying after love?

Sara Teasdale, "Spring Night"

§ PEARL BUCK *pearl of great price*

Pearl Buck was born in West Virginia in 1892 to the Sydenstrickers, deeply religious people who dedicated their lives to missionary work. They chose to spread the word of Christianity in China, and Pearl spent a good portion of her girlhood there. She attended Randolph-Macon Woman's College in Virginia, but after she graduated hurried back to Asia with her teaching certificate.

She made her living as a teacher until she married John Buck, a fellow American and agriculturist. They married in 1917 and lived in northern China among the peasants. The Bucks had one child, born mentally handicapped, and adopted another child during Pearl's tenure at the University of Nanking. In 1922, she started writing during the long hours she spent caring for her ailing mother. Her very first story was published in *Asia* magazine three years later. Pearl Buck returned to the United States to seek proper care for her daughter and studied for her master's degree at Cornell. Later, she taught at three different universities in China, until anti-foreigner sentiments became unavoidable. Fleeing violence in 1927, Pearl lost the manuscript for her first novel. Still, she continued, publishing *East Wind: West Wind* in 1930, followed the next year by *The Good Earth*.

The Good Earth was a global phenomenon from the beginning, winning the Pulitzer Prize in 1932. A stage play was also written and a script for the Academy Award-winning film. Pearl Buck was a huge success, seeing her book translated into dozens of languages and selling millions of copies. While her success was generally more popular than critical, that all changed when, in 1938, she became the first American woman to win the Nobel Prize. In 1935, she left her adopted country, divorced her husband, and returned to the United States. Soon after, she married her publisher, Richard J. Walsh, and continued to write novels and articles until her death.

Buck was an amazingly prolific writer, once writing five books in one year and penning more than eighty-five in all. Her work includes plays, biographies, books for children, translations, and autobiography as well as novels. During the McCarthy years, she came under suspicion and was forced to write under the pseudonym John Sedges, but she never ceased in her essential beliefs of tolerance and understanding.

She founded the East and West Association and was the president of the Author's Guild, a free speech organization founded in the 1950s. She also created an organization to care for orphans

PEARL BUCK *This West Virginia girl became a crusader for global relations and the first American woman to receive the Nobel Prize in Literature.*

of Asian mothers and American fathers and adopted six such children herself. A champion of women's rights and rights for the mentally handicapped, she died of lung cancer in 1973 in her home of Danby, Vermont. She was a fierce crusader for greater mutual understanding for the people of the world and, with her Nobel Prize in Literature, opened a new chapter for women in literature.

(I want to) write for the people. . . .

Pearl S. Buck, regarding her great novel *The Good Earth*

GWENDOLYN BROOKS *poet of the Beat*

Gwendolyn Brooks has the distinction of being the first black person to receive the Pulitzer Prize (for *Annie Allen* in 1950). One of the most innovative poets in the literary landscape of America, she was born in 1917 in Topeka, Kansas. But her family moved when she was young to the more urban city of Chicago, which imparted a street-smart influence that still informs her work. Brooks wanted to bring poetry to the poor black kids of the inner city, attracting them with rapid-fire, tightly wound iambic pentameter that predated rap. In later life, she took a more radical bent, hooking up with the revolutionary black Beat writer LeRoi Jones (now Amiri Baraka) and Don L. Lee, and jumping into the causes of African Americans with both feet. She became a tough and angry Black Power poet, penning verses grounded in classical style deconstructed through the lens of her newfound racial awareness and commitment to cause. Forty years after her prize-winning feat, her poetry is still raw, fresh, and commanding.

I want to clarify my language. I want these poems to be free. I want them to be direct without sacrificing the kind of music, the picture-making I've always been interested in. —Gwendolyn Brooks

§ GRAZIA DELEDDA *songs of Sardinia*

While Pearl Buck and *The Good Earth* are household names, the Italian novelist Grazia Deledda is much less familiar. But she received the Nobel Prize for literature twelve years before Buck and was a powerful voice among her people.

Born in 1871 in Sardinia, Deledda was a country girl who had little exposure to formal education. She did have access to books, however, and read avidly. She came from a troubled clan and was seemingly the only family member to escape illness or criminality, thus bearing the brunt of household chores and responsibility. Still, she managed to write in her precious spare time.

She married in 1900, and with her new husband moved to Rome, where she sought a broader readership for her work. She soon received approval from the critics and began writing intently, striving for excellence, writing what she knew best—stories of the life and passions of the peasants of Sardinia, in her words, a place of "myths and legends." Deledda was dedicated to her craft and produced a considerable body of work, including her favorite novel, *Canne al vento (Reeds in the Wind)*, the story of a dissolute family centered around the guilt of a servant, and *La Madre (The Mother)*, about the turbulent relationship between a mother and her son. In addition to her novels and short stories, she produced one volume of poetry, *Paesaggi sardi (Sardinian Landscapes)*, a translation of Balzac, and a nonfiction analysis of the customs of her native island.

She was awarded the Nobel Prize in 1926, the first Italian woman to be so honored. She died ten years later, and her autobiography *Cosima* was published posthumously the next year.

LUTIE EUGENIA STERNS *librarian extraordinary*

In 1887, Lutie Sterns began teaching in the Milwaukee school system. She quickly became appalled at the paucity of books for her students and made such use of the public library for her kids that library officials offered her the job of superintendent of the circulation department. Lutie's passion for the public library system would lead her to travel the state indefatigably by train, boat, buggy, and sleigh, preaching the importance of public libraries and, according to legend, wearing out five fur coats in the process. This was no easy feat—Lutie had a bad stammer, but she cared so much for the cause that she wrote her speeches to avoid the letters she had trouble with. Before she "retired" to campaign for women's suffrage and child labor protection, she had established 101 free libraries and 1,480 traveling libraries in the state of Wisconsin.

§ GABRIELA MISTRAL *voice of the people*

A poor, rural schoolteacher of mixed race, Gabriela Mistral went on to become the first Latin American woman to win a Nobel Prize in Literature. She was born in the Chilean village of Montegrande in 1889. Her mother, Petronila Alcayaga, of Basque descent, was a teacher, and her father, Jeronimo Villanueva, also a teacher, was a gypsy poet of Indian and Jewish birth. Jeronimo was overly fond of wine and not quite so attached to his duties as a breadwinner and father; he deserted the family when Gabriela was three. As a schoolgirl, Gabriela discovered her call to poetry and also tapped into her own stubborn independence, switching her birth name, Lucila, for her choice, Gabriela. As an adult, she also chose a fitting surname, Mistral, hinting of a fragrant Mediterranean wind.

31

Her first love was a hopelessly romantic railroad worker who killed himself when the relationship faltered after two years. Her first book of poetry, *Sonetas de la Muerta (Sonnets of Death)* was written as result of her sadness, guilt, and pain over the death of this man. In 1914, she received Chile's top prize for poetry.

In the '20s and '30s, she wrote many volumes of poetry including *Desolacion (Desolation)*, *Ternura (Tenderness)*, *Questions*, *Tala*, and a mixed-media anthology, *Readings for Women*. In addition to writing and teaching, Mistral felt a special sympathy for women and children and worked to help victims of World Wars I and II. She made social strides as an educator as well. She initiated programs for schooling the poor, founded a mobile library system, and traveled the world, gleaning whatever information she could to improve Chile's education system. In 1923, she was named "Teacher of the Nation." She became an international envoy and ambassador off and on for her country for twenty years, eventually serving in the League of Nations and the United Nations.

In the late 1920s, a military government seized power in Chile and offered Mistral an ambassadorship to all the nations of Central America. Mistral refused to work for the military state and made a scathing public denouncement of the government machine. Her pension was revoked and Mistral had to support herself, her mother, and her sister through her writing. She lived in exile for a while in

GABRIELA MISTRAL *Chile's "Teacher of the Nation" and Nobel poet.*

France, eventually moving to the United States, where she taught at Middlebury and Barnard Colleges, and at the University of Puerto Rico.

In 1945 she received the Nobel Prize. Upon accepting the revered award, Gabriela Mistral, in her plain black velvet, made a sharp contrast with Sweden's dashing King Gustav. Pointedly, she didn't accept the prize for herself, but on behalf of the "poets of my race." Mistral died in 1957, mourned by her native Chile, where she was revered as a national treasure. She was the "people's poet," giving voice to the humble people to whom she belonged—the Indians, mestizos, and Campesanos—and scorning the rampant elitism and attempts at creating a racial hierarchy in Europe and in her beloved Chile.

> *I consider myself to be among the children of that twisted thing that is called a racial experience, or better, a racial violence.*
>
> Garbriela Mistral
> _____

§ LORRAINE HANSBURY *young, gifted, and black*

Chicago native Lorraine Hansberry was born in 1930 to a politically aware and progressive family who knew that they had to work to make the changes they wished to see. But they paid a price. When Lorraine was only five, she got a white fur coat for Christmas and was beaten up when she wore it to school. In 1938, the black family moved to Hyde Park, an exclusive and exclusively white neighborhood. Lorraine's memories of first living in that house are of violence—being spit on, cursed at, and having bricks thrown though the windows. Her mother Nannie kept a gun with her inside the house in case it got any worse. An Illinois court evicted them, but her real estate broker father hired NAACP attorneys and had the decision overturned at the Supreme Court level, winning a 1940 landmark victory. He died at a relatively young age, which Lorraine ascribed to the pressure of the long struggle for civil rights.

Lorraine Hansbury's parents' work as activists brought them into contact with the black leaders of the day. She was well accustomed to seeing luminaries such as Langston Hughes, Paul Robeson, and W. E. B. DuBois in her home. Educated in the segregated public schools of the time, she attended the University of Wisconsin at Madison before she moved to New York for "an education of another kind."

Throughout her life, she stayed dedicated to the values her parents had instilled in her and worked steadfastly for the betterment of black people. At a picket line protesting the exclusion of black athletes from college sports, Lorraine met the man she would marry, a white Jewish liberal, Robert Nemiroff. Lorraine worked for Paul Robeson's radical black newspaper *Freedom* until her husband's career as a musician and songwriter earned enough to support them so that Lorraine could write full time.

Her first play, *A Raisin in the Sun,* was a huge hit, winning the New York Drama Critics' Circle Award as Best Play of the Year in 1959. Hansbury was the youngest American and the first black person to receive this prize. This proved to be a watershed event; after the success of *A Raisin in the Sun,* black actors and writers entered the creative arts in a surge. Lorraine continued to write plays, but in 1963 was diagnosed with cancer. She died six years after winning the Drama Critics' Award, at the age of thirty-four, tragically cutting short her work. Nevertheless, she made huge strides with her play, forever changing "the Great White Way."

> *Racism is a device that, of itself, explained nothing.*
> *It is simply a means, An invention to justify the rule*
> *of some men over others.*

From *Les Blancs: The Collected*
Last Plays of Lorraine Hansberry

---

§ BARBARA TUCHMAN *making history*

One of the most respected historians of the twentieth century and the only woman to win a Pulitzer Prize twice, Barbara Tuchman has written first-rate chronicles accessible to readers from every walk of

---

SELMA LAGERLÖf AND NELLY SACHS *Nobel nobility*

In 1909, Selma Lagerlöf became the first woman and the first Swedish writer to receive the Nobel Prize in Literature. The prize was awarded for her body of work, including the 1891 novel *To the Story of Gösta Berling* and the 1902 two-volume work of fiction *Jerusalem,* the chronicle of Swedish peasants who migrated to Jerusalem. Selma was the preeminent Swedish writer of her day and produced an impressive body of work-thirty novels and four biographical narratives. She wasn't content merely to be the most brilliant novelist of her age, however; she also worked extremely hard at obtaining the release of Jewish writer Nelly Sachs from a Nazi concentration camp. Sachs, inspired by her savior, won the Nobel Prize in Literature herself in 1966!

❦ ❦ ❦ ❦ ❦ ❦ ❦ ❦ ❦

life. The core of her theory of history is that true understanding comes from observing the patterns that are created through an aggregation of details and events. Tuchman has covered topics from the Trojan War to the Middle Ages, the leaders of World War I, and the United State's problematic involvement in Vietnam. All of her books are known for their narrative power and her portrayals of the players on the world stage as believable individuals.

Born in 1912, Barbara Tuchman attended Radcliffe College and after graduation took her first job as a research assistant at the Institute of Pacific Relations in New York and Tokyo. She began writing articles for several periodicals and went on to work as a staff editorial assistant at the *Nation* and a correspondent of London's *New Statesmen*. From 1934 to 1945, Tuchman worked for the Far East News Desk and Office of War Information. Here, she got firsthand experience researching and writing about history as it happened.

BARBARA TUCHMAN *Chronicler of the world's history and the only woman to receive the Pulitzer Prize twice.*

Tuchman put this invaluable wartime experience to good use with her immense study of the pivotal events prior to World War I, *The Guns of August,* published in 1962. This thoughtful and thorough history of the thirty days leading up to the first global war spanned all of Europe, detailing the actions of key players in London, Berlin, St. Petersburg, and Paris. Her book was met with thundering critical praise and acceptance from popular readers and historians the world over—she received her first Pulitzer Prize for this powerful exposé.

Barbara Tuchman's other books include *A Distant Mirror,* which explores everyday life in fourteenth-century France, and *The March of Folly,* an analysis of four conflicts in world history that were mismanaged by governments, from the Trojan War to Britain's loss of her colonies and Vietnam. Her second Pulitzer Prize was for a biography of U.S. General Joseph Stilwell, a probing look at the relations between China and the United States through the personal wartime experiences of Stilwell.

> *To be a bestseller is not necessarily a measure of quality, but it is a measure of communication.*
>
> Barbara Tuchman

—————————

§ RACHEL CARSON *"The Natural World . . . Supports All Life"*

World-famous pioneering ecologist and science writer Rachel Carson turned nature writing on its head. Before she came along, notes Women Public Speakers in the United States, "the masculine orientation [to the subject] emphasized either the dominant, aggressive encounter of humanity with wild nature or the distancing of nature through scientific observation." By creating a different, more feminine relationship to nature, Rachel Carson portrayed humans as part of the great web of life, separate only in our ability to destroy it. In a very real sense, Rachel Carson not only produced the first widely read books on ecology, but laid the foundation for the entire modern environmental movement.

Rachel inherited her love of nature from her mother, Maria, a naturalist at heart, who took Rachel for long walks in woods and meadows. Born in 1907, Rachel was raised on a farm in Pennsylvania, where the evidence of industry was never too far away. By the beginning of the twentieth century, Pennsylvania had changed a great deal from the sylvan woodlands named for colonial William Penn. Coal and strip mines had devastated some of the finest farmland. Chemical plants, steel mills, and hundreds of factories were belching pure evil into the air.

As she grew, Rachel's love of nature took an unexpected turn toward oceanography, a budding science limited by technological problems for divers. The young girl was utterly fascinated by this biological science, and though she majored in English and loved to write, she heard the ocean's siren song increasingly. While studying at the Pennsylvania College for Women in the middle 1920s, she changed her major to zoology, despite the overwhelming advice of her professors to stay the course in English, a much more acceptable major for a young woman. Her advisors were quite correct in their assertions that women were blocked from science; there were very few teaching positions except at the handful of women's colleges, and even fewer job prospects for women outside of academia.

However, Rachel listened to her heart and graduated with high honors, a fellowship to study at Woods Hole Marine Biological Laboratory for the summer, and a full scholarship to Johns Hopkins University in Maryland to study marine zoology. Rachel's first semester in graduate school coincided with the beginning of the Great Depression. Her family lost their farm; her parents and brother came to live with her in her tiny campus apartment. She helped make ends meet with part-time teaching at Johns Hopkins and the University of Maryland, while continuing her studies.

In 1935, Rachel's father suffered a heart attack and died quite suddenly. Rachel looked desperately for work to support her mother and brother, but no one would hire a woman as a full-time university science professor. Brilliant and hardworking, Rachel was encouraged to teach grade school or, better yet, be a housewife, because it was "inappropriate" for women to work in science.

Finally, her unstinting efforts to work in her field were ultimately rewarded by a job writing radio scripts for Elmer Higgins at the United States Bureau of Fisheries—a perfect job for her because it combined her strength in writing with her scientific knowledge. Then a position opened up at the bureau for a junior aquatic biologist. The job was to be awarded to the person with the highest score: Rachel aced the test and got the position. Elmer Higgins saw that her writing was excellent, making science accessible to the general public. At his direction, she submitted an essay about the ocean to the *Atlantic Monthly,* which not only published Rachel's piece, but asked her to freelance for them on a continuing basis, resulting in a book deal from a New York publishing house.

By now, Rachel was the sole support of her mother, brother, and two nieces. She raised the girls, supported her mother, and worked a demanding, full-time job, leaving her research and writing to weekends and late nights. But she prevailed nonetheless. Her first book, *Under the Sea Wind,* debuted in 1941 to a war-preoccupied public. It was a completely original book, enacting a narrative of the seacoast with the flora and fauna as characters, the first indication of Rachel's unique perspective on nature.

Rachel's second book, *The Sea Around Us,* was a nonfiction presentation of the relationship of the ocean to earth and its inhabitants. This time, the public was ready and she received the National Book Award and made the *New York Times* bestseller list for nearly two years. *The Edge of the Sea* was also very well received, both critically and publicly. Rachel Carson's message of kinship with all life combined with a solid foundation of scientific knowledge found an audience in postwar America. However, shy and solitary, Rachel avoided the literary spotlight by accepting a grant that allowed her to return to her beloved seacoast, where she could often be found up to her ankles in mud or sand, researching.

As her popularity rose and her income from book royalties flooded in, Rachel was able to quit her job and build a coastal cottage for herself and her mother. She also returned the grant money that had been given her, asking it be redistributed to needy scientists. In 1957, a letter from one of Rachel's readers would change everything. The letter came from Olga Owens Huckins, who was reporting the death of birds after airplanes sprayed dichloro-diphenyl-trichloroethane (DDT), a chemical then in heavy use. Carson was keenly interested in discovering the effects of DDT on the natural habitat. Her findings were shocking: if birds and animals weren't killed outright by DDT, its effects were even more insidious—thin eggshells broke before the hatchlings were fully developed. DDT was also suspected of being carcinogenic to humans.

Rachel vowed to write a book about the devastating impact of DDT upon nature "or there would be no peace for me," she proclaimed. Shortly after, she was diagnosed with cancer. Despite chemotherapy, surgery, and constant pain, Rachel worked slowly and unstintingly on her new book. In 1962, *Silent Spring* was published. It was like a cannon shot. Chemical companies fought back, denied, and ran for cover against the public outcry. Vicious charges against Rachel were aimed at what many of the captains of the chemical industry viewed as her Achilles heel—her womanhood.

"Not a real scientist," they claimed. She was also called unstable, foolish, and sentimental for her love of nature. With calm logic and cool reason, Rachel Carson responded in exacting scientific terms, explaining the connections among DDT, the water supply, and the food chain.

Ultimately, President John F. Kennedy assigned his Science Advisory Committee the task of examining the pesticide, and Rachel Carson was proven to be absolutely correct. She died two years later, and although her reputation continued to be maligned by the chemical industry, her books had launched a movement that continues to this day.

> *Perhaps if Dr. Rachel Carson had been Dr. Richard*
> *Carson the controversy would have been minor. . . .*
> *The American technocrat could not stand the pain*
> *of having his achievements deflated by the pen of*
> *this slight woman.*

Joseph B. C. White, author

---

§ BETTY FRIEDAN *mother of modern feminism*

In 1956, young housewife Betty Friedan submitted her article about the frustrations women experience in their traditional roles as housewives and mothers. She received rejections from *McCalls, The Ladies' Home Journal,* and every other publication she approached. The editors, all men in that day and age, were disapproving, going so far as to say any woman would have to be "sick" to not be completely satisfied in her rightful role!

But Betty knew that she and the millions of women like her were not sick, just stifled. Betty had put aside her dream of being a psychologist for fear of becoming a spinster, instead choosing to marry and work for a small newspaper. She was fired from her job when she got pregnant for the second time, and began, like most middle-class women of her day and age, to devote herself full-time to the work of running a home and family, what she called "the dream life, supposedly, of American women at that time."

But after a decade of such devotion, she still wasn't happy and theorized that she wasn't alone. A graduate of Smith College, she decided to poll her fellow alumnae. Most of her classmates, who had given up promising careers to devote themselves to their families, felt incomplete; many were deeply depressed. They felt guilty for not being completely content sacrificing their individual dreams for their families, each woman certain that her dissatisfaction was a personal failing. Betty called this "the problem that has no name," and she gave it one, "the feminine mystique."

Over the next five years, her rejected article evolved into a book as she interviewed hundreds of women around the country. *The Feminine Mystique* explored the issue of women's lives in depth, criticizing American advertisers' exclusively dom-

According to Alvin Toffler, BETTY FRIEDAN *"pulled the trigger of history" with her book* The Feminine Mystique.

estic portrayal of women and issuing a call to action for women to say no to the housewife role and adopt "a new life plan" in which they could have both families and careers. With its publication in 1963, *The Feminine Mystique* hit America like a thunderbolt; publisher W. W. Norton had printed only 2,000 copies, never anticipating the sale of 3 million copies in hardcover alone.

Unintentionally, Betty had started a revolution. She was flooded with letters from women saying her book gave them the courage to change their lives and decry equal access to employment opportunities and other equality issues. Ultimately, the response to Betty's challenge created the momentum that led to the formalization of the second wave of the U.S. women's movement in 1966 with the organization of NOW, the National Organization for Woman.

Betty was NOW's first president and took her role as a leader in the women's movement seriously, traveling to lectures and campaigns for change, engendering many of the freedoms women now enjoy. She pushed for equal pay for equal work, equal job opportunities, and access to birth control and legalized abortion. In 1970, she quit NOW to fight for the Equal Rights Amendment and, in 1975, was named Humanist of the Year. Of her, author Barbara Seaman wrote, "Betty Friedan is to the women's movement what Martin Luther King was to blacks."

In 1981, responding to critics who claimed feminism ignored the importance of relationships and families to most women, she penned *The Second Stage,* in which she called on men and women to work together to make the home and the workplace havens for both genders. These days, Betty is making another revolution with her latest book, *The Fountain of Age,* raising consciousness about society's stereotypes about aging thirty years after she, as futurist

Alvin Toffler so aptly put it, "pulled the trigger of history" with *The Feminine Mystique.*

It's been a lot of fun making the revolution.

Betty Friedan

§ TONI MORRISON *the truest eye*

Toni Morrison comes from small-town, working-class Ohio, a state that fell "between" the Civil War issue of slavery, a state with many stops along the underground railroad, and a state where many crosses burned "neither plantation nor ghetto." She has made this her canvas for her rich, original stories that dare tell uncomfortable truths. And for her daring she won the Nobel Prize in Literature.

Born in 1931 as Chloe Anthony Wofford, Toni and her parents worked hard as sharecroppers in their adopted northern home of Lorain, Ohio. She was keenly interested in language as a child and loved hearing ghost stories, songs, and thundering sermons at church. After high school, she attended Howard University, graduating at the age of twenty-two, and followed that with a master's program at Cornell. Her thesis paper examined the theme of suicide in the works of Virginia Woolf and William Faulkner. She began teaching at Howard and met and married a Jamaican architect, Harold Morrison, with whom she had two sons, Harold Ford and Slade. The marriage was short-lived, and Toni took the children and moved to Syracuse and later, New York City, where she was hired by Random House as senior editor. She worked on several major black autobiographies of the time, including those of Black Power revolutionary

44

Angela Davis and world champion boxer Muhammad Ali.

As a writer, Toni Morrison made an immediate mark upon America's literary landscape with *The Bluest Eye,* published in 1970, and *Sula,* published three years later. Her next book, *Song of Solomon,* won the national Book Critics' Circle Award in 1978. In 1983, she left Random House to devote herself full time to writing and spent the next five years writing *Beloved,* the fantastical and tragic story of ex-slave Sethe and her children.

Her writing focuses on black women who had previously been ignored. Her lyrical language combines with both realistic and mythic plot elements to create a distinctive style all her own. In 1993, Morrison won the Nobel Prize in Literature; she was the first black American to do so. She said, "I am outrageously happy. But what is most wonderful for me, personally, is to know that the prize has been awarded to an African-American. Winning as an American is very special— but winning as a black American is a knock-out."

> *Had I loved the life that the state planned for me*
> *from the beginning, I would have lived and died in*
> *somebody else's kitchen.*

> Toni Morrison in a speech to the
> International Literary Congress in New York

two

Ink in Their Veins

Theories of Relativity

SOME WOMEN seem to have writing talent encoded in their DNA. This is especially true of several "literary dynasties" wherein several family members are extraordinarily gifted, each with a voice uniquely his or her own. How does this happen? Do the gods (and goddesses) look down from above and occasionally say, "Hmmm, let's endow this family with writing genius through the end of time"? Or, can a special relationship with the Muses can be arranged and "passed down" from generation to generation?

Certainly, these creative kin have some strange magic in remarkable quantity. To wit, just two examples: the

49

legacy of the Brontë lineage hasn't faded with time; new editions of books and films of *Jane Eyre* and *Wuthering Heights* are released every few years like clockwork. Stateside, their doppelgängers, the Grimké sisters, were stirring up hot controversy with virulent abolition texts that helped ignite the Civil War.

Bonded by blood and shelved side by side, the women profiled here are invariably very different from each other. But they all have one thing in common: a love of the written word.

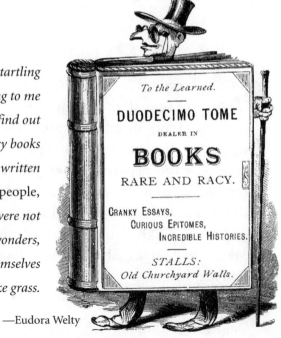

It had been startling and disappointing to me to find out that story books had been written by people, that books were not natural wonders, coming up of themselves like grass.

—Eudora Welty

§ THE BRONTËS *scribbling sisters*

The Brontë sisters were originally a troupe of five girls born in the early 1800s in a rural parsonage in Yorkshire, England. Maria and Elizabeth died before they reached the age of ten, Emily and Anne lived to adulthood, and Charlotte outlived them all. Emily Brontë tends to be the most beloved in the family, but Anne and Emily had much in common. They also had many differences; their personalities could not have been more dissimilar. And all three aspired to be writers.

Ink in Their Veins
Theories of Relativity

To make family dynamics even more complex, father Reverend Patrick Brontë, a failed writer himself, saw Emily as a genius, Charlotte very talented, and Anne not worthy of attention. The truth is, however, that the self-absorbed and somewhat silly patriarch had a staggering amount of talent under his roof. To have one daughter become a famous writer is amazing enough, but to have three is almost unimaginable.

The reverend proved more successful in theatrics, at least at home. In constant possession of a pistol, he shot though the open door if irritated and took a knife to one of his wife's silk dresses. When his wife died in 1821, he sent for his sister-in-law to care for the six children (there was one brother, Branwell). A few years later, all the girls except Anne were sent to boarding school, a horrible experience of physical deprivation; this is where the two oldest girls died. After their sisters' deaths, Charlotte and Emily were sent home.

Typically for the period, Reverend Brontë pinned his hope on his son, Branwell, an aspiring artist. Branwell was sent to university in London to pursue his dreams and failed miserably. Instead, he squandered his tuition and allowance on gin. When he had run through all of the money, he returned home, telling lies about having been robbed. The sisters ended up as teachers and governesses, but their passion was always writing.

In 1845, Charlotte discovered that Anne and Emily had been writing verse, as had she. She collected them into one volume and published it herself, using the male pseudonyms—Currer (Charlotte), Ellis (Emily), and Acton (Anne) Bell—that they would retain throughout their careers. The book sold one copy. Not to be deterred, they all continued writing. Soon they were publishing to great acclaim.

Charlotte Brontë's *Jane Eyre* achieved spectacular success during her lifetime, and it has survived the test of time, retold again and again in films. She also penned the well-received novels *Shirley* and *Vilette.* Anne's *Agnes Gray* and *The Tenant of Wildfell Hall* are less known now, but were critical and popular successes in their day.

CHARLOTTE BRONTË *Author of* Jane Eyre, *sister of Emily Brontë; the two were the "muses of the moors."*

But it is Emily who is considered by critics to be the literary genius of the family, based on her poems and her opus *Wuthering Heights,* which shone with a brilliance and sense of drama and mystery nearly unmatched in all of English literature. Family and friends marveled that sweet-natured Emily, always cleaning and ironing, was capable of the volcanic passions and drama she unleashed in her tale of love on the moors. Her Heathcliff is a brute, a primal presence as wild as the wind, a perfect foil for the spoiled, difficult Catherine. When it came out that the author was a woman, some critics of the day declared that *Wuthering Heights* must actually be the work of Branwell, on the grounds that no woman, particularly one who led such a sheltered existence, could have written such a passionate book.

Emily and Anne died young (at her brother's funeral, Emily caught the cold that would eventually kill her). Charlotte went on to be lionized as a literary giant and hobnobbed with the likes of William Makepeace Thackeray, Mrs. Gaskell, and Matthew Arnold. She married her father's curate in 1854 and died the following year.

> *I'll walk where my own nature would be leading:*
> *It vexes me to choose another guide.*
>
> Emily Brontë

§ ALICE JAMES *sibling rivalry*

Baby sister to brainy overachievers William and Henry James, Alice James, born in 1848, was also a writer of intensity and introspection. But she suffered greatly as a product of the Victorian Age: her brothers were the recipients of all the glory and Alice was relegated to the house. Given the times, despite her great familial connections, Alice had little chance of publication and gradually receded into the shadows of her brothers' gargantuan reputations as geniuses in philosophy and fiction.

Alice was sick her whole adult life. Sadly, it seems that her frustrations about career and gender contributed to her illness and neurasthenia. She had her first spells at sixteen and was given a regimen of treatments involving "blistering baths," electricity treatments, and sulfuric, ether, and motor therapy sessions. These medical advancements didn't seem to help so much as harm her, and she was depressed and suicidal by the age of thirty. Her father, a Christian mystic preacher and ambitious intellectual, magnanimously gave her "permission" to die, which lessened her interest in that option. The more sensitive sibling, novelist Henry James, noted that "in our family group girls seem scarcely to have had a chance" and that his sister's "tragic health was, in a manner, the only solution for her of the practical problems of life." Alice and her long-time companion Katherine Peabody were the models for Henry James novel about a pair of suffragist lovers in *The Bostonians*.

Despite her ill health, she did manage to keep a diary. Published after her death, it is now regarded as a seminal text in nineteenth-century feminist studies and a window into the world of invalidism. Nearly forgotten until the mid-1980s, Alice James has recently come to the attention of critics: a volume of her letters and an in-depth biography recognize her as a "silenced" voice of her era and tell a tragic tale of a woman trapped in a time in which a role as wife was the only real choice for women. Her long period of decay and isolation led her to view her eventual death from breast cancer as a respite from a torturous existence that offered no option to exercise her talent or will.

A written monologue by that most interesting being,
myself, may have its yet to be discovered consola-

*tions. I shall at least have it all my own way and it
may bring relief as an outlet to that geyser of emotions, sensations, speculations, and reflections which
ferments perpetually. . . .*

From *The Diary of Alice James*

---

§ AMY LOWELL *"maker of fine poems"*

Sometimes, a strong woman following her own distinct destiny
becomes better known for her strength of personality and the
celebrity surrounding it than for her actual accomplishments. Amy
Lowell is just such a person.

Born in 1874 at the tail end of the Gilded Age, she came from
a family of accomplished intellectuals and writers, cousin to the
legendary New England poets James Russell Lowell and Robert
Lowell and nearly every other male running MIT or Harvard. As a
girl, she agonized over her weight and, despite desperate and severe
diets, couldn't surmount that personal issue. Her fears about her
ability to fit in led to "nervous prostrations," but her love of the
written word kept her going. "I am ugly, fat, conspicuous & dull,"
she wrote in her diary at the age of fifteen. "I should like best of
anything to be literary."

Though she was, in her own right, a skilled critic and fine poet,
her recognition came in a large part for her eccentricities—in particular, wearing tailored men's suits, smoking cigars, and keeping a
pack of dogs. Her original approach to appearance and personal
habits certainly extended to her writing and, after her first tradi-
tionally lyric book of poetry in 1912, *A Dome of Many-Colored Glass*,

she began working in the pioneering modernist and imagist style brought to international attention by Ezra Pound, H. D., and T. S. Eliot.

Indeed, Amy Lowell cited H. D. as a major influence on her open verse and cadence, what she referred to as "polymorphic prose." Her more experimental work, done after 1913, has come to be regarded as her best. She also had a fascination with Asian art, poetry, and aesthetics, publishing in 1921 *Fir-Flower Tablets*, a group of original poems combined with avant garde translations of Chinese poetry in collaboration with Florence Ayscough. A powerfully insightful literary critic, she also lectured, compiled anthologies of poetry by H. D. and others, and completed an immense biography of the great English poet John Keats.

Part of her legacy as a writer includes a group of love poems called *The Letter and Madonna of the Evening Flowers,* inspired by her lover and companion Ada Dwyer Russell. After her parents' deaths, Amy invited Ada to live with her in their baronial mansion in a manner that caused several to compare them to the Paris-bound duo Gertrude Stein and Alice B. Toklas.

AMY LOWELL *Cigar-smoking critic and Imagist poet, or, as Ezra Pound put it, "Amygist."*

Indeed, they had the same relational dynamic, with former actress Russell playing Toklas' role as cook, nurse, and companion. Ada was no mere muse however; the two worked together and sparked each other's creativity. Amy even talked about hanging up a shingle outside her family mansion, Sevenels, saying "Lowell & Russell, Makers of Fine Poems."

Amy Lowell also pursued her poetic vision by traveling to meet others and sought out Ezra Pound, Henry James, D. H Lawrence, H. D., Robert Frost, and John Gould Fletcher, with whom she forged lasting friendships. The success of her imagist masterpieces *Can Grande's Castle* and *Pictures of the Floating World* prompted Ezra Pound, ostensibly the founder of that movement, to start calling the radial new style, "Amygism." In 1925, she wrote *What O'Clock,* which won a Pulitzer Prize for poetry after her death that year from a cerebral hemorrhage.

> *Little cramped words scrawling all over the paper*
> *Like draggled fly's legs.*
> *What can you tell of the flaring moon?*
> *Through the oak leaves?*

> Amy Lowell, from "The Letter"

§ MARY SHELLEY *Gothic greatness*

Nearly everyone in Mary Shelley's life was a writer. Her mother Mary Wollstonecraft was one of the first feminist writers and thinkers; her father William Godwin wrote philosophical theory. Their home in England was a regular gathering place for the radical elite; Charles Lamb and Samuel Coleridge were among their regular visitors. Politically, her parents were revolutionaries who disapproved of marriage, but went through with the legalities to legitimize Mary upon her birth in 1797. Mary Wollstonecraft died eleven days after the baby was born, and Godwin fell apart, neglecting his daughter terribly, perhaps blaming her for his beloved wife's death. He later remarried and let relatives, nannies, and his new wife take whatever care of Mary they chose. Mary recalls learning to write by tracing her mother's name on her gravestone at her father's urging.

At seventeen, Mary met the married playboy poet Percy Bysshe Shelley and ran away with him to Europe, returning after a few weeks to London, drowning in debt. By 1816, the couple had a more secure financial footing and headed for the continent again, this time to Switzerland's Lake Geneva, to a party with Shelley's friend Lord Byron. A bout of ghost stories told around the fire as a distraction from an unusually cold summer inspired nineteen-year-old Mary to pick up a pen. Written in one year, *Frankenstein* is now hailed as the first Gothic novel and a seminal work of science fiction.

In 1818, *Frankenstein* was published, and Mary and Percy Shelley returned to London and married after the death of his wife. What proved to be a watershed year for the pair because of the publication of her book was an extremely difficult one; Mary's half-sister Fanny and Percy Shelley's wife both committed suicide. Their marriage was met with extreme disapproval and the newlyweds fled to Italy to escape the controversy. Mary had three children; all but one, a son, died. Mother and son survived husband and father, when, in 1822, an exiled Shelley and fellow rebel poets drowned in the Bay of Spezia in Italy.

His young widow and surviving son were left behind, virtually
destitute. Mary managed to scratch out a living to support her

father and two-year-old child, but was an outcast from society. Mary wrote other romances, including *The Last Man, Lodore,* and *Valperga,* but none reached the level of success or acclaim of her first. She idolized her late husband and memorialized him in her fiction, in addition to editing the first published volume of his poetry in 1839. Mary Shelley died in 1851 of a brain tumor. Now, more than 150 years after her death, the book she wrote at the age of nineteen continues to inform, inspire, and amaze.

Ink in Their Viens
Theories of Relativity

My imagination, unbidden, possessed and guided me.

Mary Shelley, from *Frankenstein*

MARY WOLLSTONECRAFT *feminist firecracker*

Though her life was troubled and turbulent, Mary has gone down in history as a major contributor to feminist literature. Her works, *Thoughts on the Education of Daughters,* written in 1787, and *A Vindication of the Rights of Woman* (1793) are lucid and forward-thinking, touchstones in gender studies. Born in 1759, Wollstonecraft worked for a London publisher, James Johnson, which bolstered her independence, but she left for Paris in order to see the French Revolution for herself. As a cover, she passed herself off as the daughter of American captain Gilbert Imlay, with whom she became involved, producing a daughter, Fanny. The affair broke up and a brokenhearted Mary tried unsuccessfully to kill herself; ironically, her daughter Fanny would later succeed at suicide. She went back to London and her old publishing job in 1795. James Johnson had become involved with an extremist political group comprised of Thomas Paine, William Wordsworth, William Godwin, Thomas Holcraft, and William Blake. Mary and Godwin fell in love and she became pregnant with Mary.

At the turn of the twentieth century, Erica Jong's daughter Molly has taken up her pen and shows no fear of flying, while siblings Eliza and Susan Minot are authoring critically acclaimed novels and nonfiction and, to their mutual enjoyment, witnessing the shock of readers and listeners who marvel at how "different" they are, as people and as writers.

w w w w w w

§ DOROTHY WORDSWORTH *"wild lights in her eyes"*

Beloved poet William Wordsworth was one of his sister's biggest admirers and she his "dearest friend" during his life. She was the only girl of the five children born to the Dorsetshire family. When their mother passed away in 1778, when Dorothy was seven, relatives raised her away from her four brothers.

But despite being raised apart, William and Dorothy were extremely close. William, two years older than his sister, inherited some money of his own when he turned twenty-six and bought an English country cottage just for the two of them. William's destiny as a poet was already unfolding. Dorothy, to aid her brother and amuse him, began to keep a series of journals that not only reveal the lives of important literary figures but also have a purity and merit all their own. The portraits of their daily existence alone are priceless, but her machinations to inspire and "preserve" her brother as a poet are also remarkable. Today scholars pour over the journals for their wealth of information about the poet.

When William met and married Mary Hutchinson, at first Dorothy felt betrayed and abandoned. Eventually, her loyalty and love won out, and she pitched in to care for his children, for whom she wrote her own poetry, including "Peaceful Is Our Valley." The valley in which they lived, rhapsodized over by brother William, was peaceful indeed, an idyll visited often by friends William Hazlitt, Robert Southey, Charles Lamb, Thomas De Quincey, Samuel Coleridge, and Robinson. De Quincey penned reminiscences about his visits to the cottage where he was shocked by what he perceived as Dorothy stepping outside a proper feminine role: "The exclusive character of her reading, and the utter want of pretension, and of all that looks like bluestockingisms."

Later writers, including Virginia Woolf, puzzled over her life: Was she stifled by the towering talent of her brother and held back by her gender? A closer look at her diaries and the beautifully sculpted entries there reveal one thing certainly: she was a happy person and one with nature and her own nature. While her brother sometimes labored over his works, under pressure to produce for the eyes of the world, she was free to allow her impressions to flow freely. However, not all was to remain rosy forever; she spent the last twenty-five years of her life struggling with both physical and mental illness.

> *The Sea perfectly calm blue, streaked with deeper*
> *colour by the clouds, and tongues or points or sand,*
> *on our return a gloomy red. The sun goes down. The*
> *crescent moon, Jupiter and Venus.*
>
> Dorothy Wordsworth

FOR MANY WOMEN WRITERS, IT TOOK A MASCULINE PEN NAME TO GET PUBLISHED

Amandine Lucie Aurore Dupin, Baronne Dudevant: The famous French novelist George Sand

Mary Ann (or Marian) Evans: The great English Victorian novelist George Eliot

Acton, Currer, and Ellis Bell: The beloved Brontës—Ann, Charlotte, and Emily respectively

Lee Chapman, John Dexter, and Morgan Ives: All *nom de plumes* of Marion Zimmer Bradley, author of *The Mists of Avalon*

Ralph Iron: The name Olive Schreiner used to write her acclaimed *The Story of a African Farm*

Frank: The name the first woman humorist in the United States, Frances Miriam Berry Witcher, used to get published.

Lawrence Hope: The pseudonym of Adele Florence Cory, a woman, according to *Womanlist* by Marjorie P. K. Weiser and Jean S. Arbeiter, "respectably married to a middle-aged British army officer in India, who wrote passionate poems in the 1890s. One described the doomed love of a married English lady for an Indian rajah in the Kasmir. When Hope's real identity was unmasked, all London was abuzz: was she telling the truth?"

three

Mystics and Madwomen

Subversive Piety

I T's AMAZING that most of the women profiled in this chapter weren't burned at the stake! They are kindred of the "first ladies of literature" in spirit, if not in soul, writing at a time when it simply wasn't seemly for women to express independent thought, to reinterpret the Bible in their own ways, or, really, to be writing at all. Most fascinating of all is the one recurring theme in many of their mystic revelations: the feminine face of God, or "God as mother." Despite decades and sometimes centuries separating these disparate mystics, their visions and revelations were similar in detail and description of a shining, goddess-like benevolent figure. Writing is a solitary venture, and these women have been

65

the most solitary of all: anchorites imprisoned in monastic cells; spinsters in rooms of their own à la Emily Dickinson; pioneer wives stuck in remote parts of the uncivilized New World; and faithfuls on pilgrimages through the most inhospitable of surroundings and circumstances. Their texts and tracts read like modern poetry—simple, spare, passionate, and beatific, in the original meaning as appropriated by the twentieth-century Beatniks.

Women who love books too much

Forward-thinking if nothing else, these women wielded their pens skillfully, unencumbered by fear of their fellow man. Saint Catherine of Siena's dictated writings and the letters she sent to prominent men of the day influenced the politics of the medieval church, while Hilda of Whitby mentored the greatest Old English poet, Caedmon. At age fifteen, neo-Gnostic Jane Lead began having visions of Sophia, "the magical woman within the soul who would bring redemption to male and female spirits alike." Indian poet-singer Mirabai became a wandering *sadhu* for her devotion to Lord Krishna, composing verse of unmatched beauty that is still sung 400 years later. These transcendental talents are, in some cases, only now finding a readership, thanks to students of women's literature and religious scholars. Superstar Sufi poet Rumi may have to make room for these ecstatic lyrists. After all, these women, too, were divinely inspired to write.

§ HILDA OF WHITBY *patron saint*

An Englishwoman born in 614 C.E., Hilda spent most of her life teaching and creating a network of monasteries and abbeys across England. In 657, a patron gave her a piece of land in Whitby, Yorkshire, on which she established the monastery that would come to be an important breeding ground for the developing scholarship and literature of the age. Populated by both men and women, who lived separately, Whitby attracted a wide group of intellectuals. Hilda herself taught the arts, medicine, grammar, music, and theology.

Mystics and Madwomen
Subversive Piety

Old English historian the Venerable Bede writes about Hilda and her crucial role as advisor to kings, noblemen, and laypeople. But she also had a lasting effect on the world of letters. Whitby had a large library, and the scribes of the monastery produced the *Life of Pope Gregory I,* one of England's earliest works of literature. Bede also tells of how the infinitely wise Abbess Hilda discovered the poetic potential of Caedmon, a lay brother who worked at the monastery, and encouraged him to write. As a result of her patronage, we have the earliest known examples of Christian poetry in Old English.

Originally a Celtic Christian, Hilda hosted the Synod of Whitby in 664, which was held to decide what direction Christianity would take. The synod voted to follow the Roman Catholic Church, and independent as she was, Hilda went with the majority.

While most women were illiterate until relatively recently, the tenth-century Anglo-Saxon noblewoman Wynflaed actually willed her books upon her death to another woman, Æthelflaed.

67

In 1700 B.C.E. **Amat-Mamu** was an Assyrian priestess-scribe who for forty years made her living in a cloister of 140 other such women. The clay tablets on which they wrote have survived to this day. Three hundred years before she and her sisterhood were recording the spiritual beliefs of the day, the priestess *Kubatum* in Ur wrote and performed ritual reenactments of holy erotic poetry such as the sweet—literally—lines incorporated into the Bible's sexy Song of Solomon: "Lion, let me give you my caresses . . . wash me with honey."

Women who love books too much

Marie de France was a French poet and the first women to write in a European vernacular. Many scholars regard her as the greatest woman writer of the medieval era because of her religious writing and short fiction, which preceded Chaucer and Boccaccio. Her identity is enshrouded in mystery, perhaps for her own protection. We hope that a modern scholar-sleuth will find this enigma a potent lure and challenge, and make her works and her identity accessible to us all.

J is believed to have been a tenth-century female Israelite of noble descent who wrote several narratives that are embedded in the Old Testament, though they were written six centuries before various scribes cobbled it together. The women she wrote about—King David's lover Bathsheba, Rebecca, and Tamar—come alive in her stories. While "J" the person remains a cipher, and a very controversial one among biblical experts, her identity and authenticity have recently been recognized by such a noteworthy as Harold Bloom, and a volume of the J writings has recently been published.

Perpetua was an early Christian Carthaginian, citizen of the Holy Roman Empire and member of the Montanist sect, who were proponents of equality for women. She converted her best friend, an African slave named Felicity, and both were jailed for soliciting their faith. In prison, Perpetua began to have visions and to write them down. Though facing death, she reaffirmed her faith in court and was executed by a combination of wild beasts and gladiators in a Roman circus. Her diary, a record of her trials and her unswerving faith, survives her.

Mystics and
Madwomen
Subversive Piety

Elizabeth Cady Stanton, a most practical mystic, wrote *The Woman's Bible,* no small feat. This powerful text is both a testament to and a feminist critique of the male bias in the Judeo-Christian tradition; some sentiments were echoed in the "Declaration of Sentiments" printed for the Seneca Falls suffragette convention of July 19, 1848. "Resolved, That woman is man's equal—was intended to be so by the Creator, and the highest good of the race demanded that she should be recognized as such."

I love inscriptions on flyleaves and notes in margins, I like the comradely sense of turning pages someone else turned, and reading passages some one long gone has called my attention to.

Bibliophile Helene Hanff, on the joys of second-hand books, from *84, Charing Cross Road*

§ HILDEGARD VON BINGEN
the "Sibyl of the Rhine"

Although her canonization was twice undertaken in the fifteenth century, 400 years after her death, sainthood was never realized for Hildegard von Bingen except for her inclusion in the Roman Martyrology. Hildegard began her life in Germany. The daughter of nobility, she discovered her calling at the age of three, when she first started having visions. Throughout her life, she had frequent incidents of trances, fits, and frenzied states of godly joy.

At eight years of age, she entered the Benedictine Convent at Disibodenberg as an anchorite. As a religious devotion, anchorites were locked in tiny cells that they could never leave, receiving food through a small hole by which they also passed their wastes. Luckily for Hildegard, her cell was already occupied by a German anchoress named Jutta, who instructed her in the classics and certain sciences, notably botany. Hildegard lived that way for seven years, until word of her amazing brilliance and religious devotion had so spread that women who wished to study with her crowded her cell, and the order allowed her to leave her cell and become a nun. Hildegard had two confidantes: her anchorite teacher and her lifelong friend and biographer, a monk named Volmar. When Jutta died, Hildegard was made abbess in 1147 and went on to found her own convent in Rupertsberg near Bingen.

Hildegard kept her visions secret until a voice told her to reveal them. She accurately prophesied a major papal event that took place nearly two hundred years later—the schism of the Catholic Church in 1378. She recorded her illuminating messages received in trance in her mystic trilogy, *Scivias,* covering the periods from 1142 to 1151, translated as *Know Thy Ways;* from 1158 to 1163, *Liber vitae meritorium (The Book of the Lives of the Worthy);* and from 1163 to 1173, *Liber divinorum operum (The Book of Divine Works).* Bernard of Clairvaux, a highly regarded religious philosopher and scholar, was deeply moved by Hildegard's work. With his imprimatur, Hildegard's reputation and influence expanded, leading her to play an important role in the affairs of Pope Eugenius III and the Holy Roman Emperor, Frederick Barbarossa. She also made four preaching tours, highly unusual for women.

A dynamic speaker and accomplished musician as well as a

writer, Hildegard also invented a cryptic language and calligraphy. Her exquisite religious prayer and verse are heavily laced with an emphasis on the feminine divine. Yet, her writing wasn't limited to mysticism; she also wrote scientific treatises ranging from geology to botany, physiology, cosmology, ethics, and pathology. Dubbed the "Sibyl of the Rhine," Hildegard von Bingen became, in her lifetime, a very famous woman. When she was elderly, she spoke of how she constantly saw a backdrop of radiance upon which her visions were projected. She called this "the shadow of living light."

In the twentieth century, both her poetry and music enjoy a wide revival, and she is a mainstay in spiritual anthologies.

> *Sophia! You of the whirling wings, circling encompassing energy of God—you quicken the world in your clasp.*
>
> Hildegard von Bingen,
> from *Antiphon for Divine Wisdom*

§ JULIAN OF NORWICH *the first Englishwoman of letters*

Julian was an anchoress in the Church of St. Julian in Norwich and was thought to have been undergoing a "rite of enclosure," a kind of burial service for the soul while in her solitary cell.

Julian became famous throughout England after she decided she had God's permission to share the details of her mystical experiences, a total of sixteen separate visions. Though she was keenly aware of her status as a woman, she felt no risk in recording these important messages from above. This remarkable series of events

71

occurred two days after she turned thirty, in the year 1372. At the time, Julian was gravely ill, but instead of concentrating on her own misery, she began to feel pity and compassion for the suffering of Christ on the cross. Her condition progressively worsened and she hovered near death, even receiving last rites. Immediately after the rites, she experienced a "sudden change" and started seeing images from another realm.

Julian's descriptions of these episodes, written in English, were published in a volume entitled *Revelations of Divine Love*. They tell of her visitations not just from Heavenly Hosts, but also from demons and Satan. She discussed God in terms of a maternal presence, in a section called "God the Mother."

Julian's *Revelations of Divine Love* was enormously popular reading, and was copied repeatedly during her lifetime and after her death. She has never been officially beatified and is honored on the "casual" feast day of May 13. She is oft acknowledged as the first Englishwoman of letters.

> *As truly as God is our Father, so truly is God our*
> *Mother . . . and so Jesus is our true Mother in nature*
> *by our first creation, and he is our true Mother in*
> *grace by his taking our created nature.*
>
> Julian of Norwich, from *Revelations of Divine Love*

§ CATHERINE OF SIENA

poet of prayer

Catherine was the twenty-fourth of twenty-five children born to Jacopo Benincasa, a craftsman who made his living dying cloth in the city of Siena. At the tender age of six, Catherine knew she wanted to devote her life to God, but didn't enter a convent as a novice until ten years later, in 1363. She became a nun in the Dominican order four years after that, and began her lifelong work helping the sick and destitute. During the plague, she and her female followers tended victims and buried the dead.

Loved and respected for her devotion (she was eventually canonized), later in her life she acted as a director to a circle of nuns as well as a spiritual minister to many people

CATHERINE OF SIENA *This nun and devotional writer cared for the sick and dying during the plague.*

from her community. She was a mystic, given to visions, and a poet, creating prayerful verse celebrating her faith and the glory of God.

Catherine was also an activist at heart, and participated in the politics of her time and place. She even went so far as to travel to Avignon to prevail upon the pope to return to the Vatican in Rome. She was always helping others and thinking of herself last, barely eating in her desire to purify her being and be closer to holiness. She flagellated herself three times a day, seeing her personal suffering as an offering in exchange for the good of the church, saying, "O eternal God accept the sacrifice of my life within this mystic body of holy Church. I have nothing to give by what you have given me."

Catherine never learned to write, but several of her fellow nuns wrote down her original verse, letters, and prayers. Those she uttered in solitude are lost to us forever. An ecstatic trance state often came over Catherine during her mediations, in which she would lie prostrate upon the ground. Other times, her words came in short bursts interchanged by lengthy silences. Often, she sang as she walked alone. Her health became very frail, probably due to starvation, and she died at the age of thirty-three, leaving a set of devotional works nearly unmatched in their innovative splendor.

There the soul dwells—like the fish in the sea and the sea in the fish.

Catherine of Siena

Fifteenth-century nuns in St. Catherine's Convent in Nuremberg, Germany, loved books so much that in less than fifty years, they grew their library from forty-six books to over six hundred, mostly by hand-copying sermons, parts of the New Testament, tracts, and records of the saints' lives.

§ SAINT TERESA OF AVILA *pierced by God*

One of a dozen children of Spanish nobles, Teresa de Cepeda y Abumada was born to a life of privilege on March 28, 1515. Upon her mother's death, when Teresa was thirteen, the girl was sent to live at a convent school. She was miserable there, and after she fell ill, her mind turned to thoughts of death and hell. Though she longed to leave the strict confines of the convent, the images of hell enabled her to keep from running away; "in servile fear" she "forced herself" to accept the nunnery.

For twenty years, she continued to battle with her will, her frail body, and the harshness of life in the cloister, aspiring to a life of devotion and spiritual growth with a Franciscan book as her only aid. Finally, she underwent a second conversion and, using "the eyes of the soul," began seeing visions with regularity. Her visions were colorful and like nothing she had ever seen before; she saw jewel-encrusted crucifixes and tiny, pretty angels, one of whom pierced her heart with a fiery, golden pin. When demons invaded her dreams, she merely threw holy water on them and they ran off. In one dream she experienced "transverberation," a golden lance from God that pierced her heart over and over. She also began to hear the voice of God sharing his hopes for her destiny.

Teresa was encouraged by the voice to found a small convent among the "discalced," the unshod, sandal-wearing reform movement of the Carmelite order. The discalced felt the Carmelite order was too soft; they believed in "holy poverty," including begging for alms in order to survive. Teresa and her fellow sisters were determined to live this ascetic life, and in 1563 they moved into the small St. Joseph's convent, where Teresa spearheaded the "barefoot" reformation, traveling under terrible conditions in a wooden cart to found seventeen more such religious communities.

She also wrote books, spiritual guides for followers of the movement. Her *Life* is still widely read and remains in print; *The Way of Perfection* and *The Interior Castle* were also met with an immediate readership. In *Uppity Women of the Renaissance,* Vicki León says that *The Interior Castle* was so well regarded that it "eventually won her the title of Doctor of the Church from the twentieth century's Pope Paul VI."

Teresa was referred to as a saint while still alive, but she ignored such approbation and, until her death in 1582, got on with the real business of life, scrubbing floors, begging alms, cooking for her sisters and converts, remarking that "the Lord walks among the pots and pans."

> *All things are passing; God never changeth; patience endureth.*
>
> Teresa of Avila, from her *Breviary*

---

§ MIRABAI *Krishna's consort*

An Indian *bhakti* or saint-poet, Mirabai (1498–1565) is the best known of all the northern Indian poets of this style. A Rajput princess by birth, she was steeped in literature and music by tutors in the court of her grandfather, Rao Dudaji.

Renowned for her sanctity, Mirabai married the crown prince of the kingdom of Mewar, but her religious feelings cause her to reject a husband-wife relationship with her royal groom. Instead, she worshiped her Lord, the incarnation of Krishna called Giridhara, whose great works included lifting a mountain. Tradition has it that the crown prince's family tried to kill Mirabai twice, and that she rejected the family's deities and the proper widow's rite of immolating herself on her husband's funeral pyre upon his death.

If these legends hold any truth, they could easily explain why Mirabai began wandering, leaving behind all semblance of a normal life and devoting herself exclusively to worship of her Lord Giridhara. Toward the time of her death, she stayed at the temple compound of Ranachora at Dvarka. Her devotional hymns, prayers, and poems are still sung all over India and have recently found their way into printed form in English.

> *Only those who have felt the knife can understand the wound. Only the jeweler knows the nature of the Jewel.*

> Mirabai

---

§ JANE LEAD *Sophia's prophet*

Jane Lead is one of those wonderful early women writers who are ripe for rescue from obscurity. She was born in 1624 in Norfolk to the Ward family, and was, in her own words, brought up and educated "like other girls." Her difference emerged when she turned fifteen and a voice began instructing her during a Christmas celebration. This was her first mystical experience. Six years later, she married William Lead, an older, distant relative, and her religious devotions went on the back burner. The couple raised four daughters, and after her husband's death in 1670, when Jane was forty-six years old, her interests returned strongly to the study of mysticism and a state she called "Spiritual Virginity." Jane had a powerful vision of Sophia, meaning "wisdom," a female aspect of God.

Jane Lead pored over the writings of the German theologian, Jacob Boehme, who was widely regarded as radical in his spiritual beliefs. Jane's convictions about the mystical way grew more fervent than ever, and she moved into the household of Dr. John Pordage, founder of an unorthodox religious sect. When Pordage passed away, Lead began to publish her own visions and beliefs with the help of a younger assistant, Dr. Francis Lee. Together they founded the Philadelphia Society, based on Boehme's doctrine.

Her writing and the intelligence shown therein were astonishing. In 1681, she wrote *The Heavenly Cloud Now Breaking*, followed by *The Enochian Walks with God* and the four-volume *A Fountain of Gardens, Watered by the Rivers of Divine Pleasure*. Similarly to the other well-known writer-mystics, her work is not deliberately feminist; it is deliberately religious, but it does contain imagery of a female presence in the soul, imbued with the power to renew and redeem both men and women.

> *This is the great Wonder to come forth, as Women Clothed with the Sun . . . with the Glove of this world under her feet . . . with a Crown beset with stars, plainly declaring that to her is given the Command and Power. . . .*
>
> Jane Lead

Mary Baker Eddy was a farm girl from Bow, New Hampshire. Born in 1821, she came from humble circumstances, belying the will and passion that would make her the author of one of the most widely read books in the world, *Christian Healing,* and the founder of Christian Science. She spent the first part of her life in poverty, and details about her life are obscured by carefully edited authorized biographies. We do know that she was keenly interested in spiritualism and wandered from one boarding house to another, seeking out those run by spiritualists. In the mythology propounded by Christian Science historians, these wanderings are likened to those of Christ. One difference worth noting, however, is that Mary Baker was receiving channeled information from the dead, while the Bible makes no mention that Jesus heard such ghostly voices.

Mystics and
Madwomen
Subversive Piety

She got married along the way and served as a medium on many occasions, holding active seances where long-dead loved ones appeared and her voice would change to sound like other voices. In an affidavit by one Mrs. Richard Hazeltine, she described Mrs. Eddy's trances: "These

MARY BAKER EDDY *This medium and self-proclaimed healer founded a religion and wrote its bible.*

communications (came) through her as a medium, from the spirit of one of the Apostles or of Jesus Christ." Mrs. Eddy soon began to practice healing and went on eventually to deny that she had anything to do with spiritualism.

Her life story is a confusing series of illnesses and cures of herself and everyone in her acquaintance, seemingly. Her dedication to her beliefs were mightily compelling to others, and her theories include such ideas as the Copernican reversal of the roles of mind and matter, man being "the image and likeness of God" and therefore "not matter." Mrs. Eddy had, among her other talents of mediumship, the ability to convince people and to lead them. She was nothing if not charismatic. She and her book have influenced and, perhaps, even healed many hundreds of thousands of people.

> *Change the mind, and the quality changes. Destroy*
> *the belief and tranquility disappears.*
>
> Mary Baker Eddy

---

§ EMILY DICKINSON *white witch of Amherst*

Emily Dickinson was one of the first female literary "superstars"—a rather unusual fate for a housebound recluse. Her brilliant, intense verse certainly created a legend for the poet, but her eccentricities added to the "glamour" in the original sense of the word, in casting a spell that has lasted well over a century. Born in 1830 on December 10 in Amherst, Massachusetts, Emily Dickinson was the second child of a strict and sober lawyer, Edward Dickinson, and a sweet-natured and shy mother, also named Emily. Emily junior also had an older brother, Austin, and a younger sister, Lavinia. By all accounts, the family was happy and prosperous, pillars of the community. Emily also benefited from a good education at Amherst Academy and at Mount Holyoke Female Seminary, one of the first women's colleges in America located, fortuitously for Emily, right outside Amherst.

It was during her year at Mount Holyoke that Dickinson showed glimmerings of the qualities that made her so different from her contemporaries. Lavinia, Emily's sister, relayed an amusing story about Emily bluffing her way through a mathematics test: "When the [geometry] examination came and [she] had never studied it, she went to the blackboard and gave such a glib exposition of imaginary figures that the dazed teacher passed her with the highest mark." And a classmate reported a shocking instance in which, when the principal of Mount Holyoke, Mary Lyons, asked "all those who wanted to be Christians to rise," Emily couldn't "honestly accede" and was the only one of all the women students present who "remained seated." This independence of will, mind, and imagination would inform her poetry and her life choices from that point on.

She left school and returned home (it is a topic of debate among

EMILY DICKINSON *agoraphobic, maybe; genius, definitely!*

her biographers as to whether evangelical pressure from this event caused Emily Dickinson to leave, and many believe that to be the reason, although Edward Dickinson also missed his elder daughter). For the rest of her life she rarely left the house and is now recognized to have been agoraphobic. She also fell victim to an eye disorder believed to have been exotropia, for which she was treated in Boston, nearly the only occasion for which she would take a trip of any kind, except for a handful of journeys with her sisters to see their father, now a congressman living part of the time in Washington, D.C.

Emily's journals indicate that she was aware that the "circumference" of her life was decreasing, after her lively girlhood of acting as hostess for her father's important parties and composing original verse for handmade greeting cards for her fellow students. As her daily existence narrowed, she began dressing only in white and seemingly embraced her new role as a mystical, poetic presence amid family and neighbors. She became such as hermit that she baked treats for the town's children and relatives and lowered them in a basket from her bedroom window, refusing to see or be seen by visitors. She only allowed the doctor to examine her as she walked past a half-open door, and wrote in a letter to her mentor, *Atlantic Monthly* editor Thomas Wentworth Higginson, "I do not cross my Father's ground to any house in town." Emily was aware of her bizarre behavior and the effect it had, referring to herself when she did appear as "manifesting" like a ministering priestess with her token offerings of flowers, wine, and sweet cakes.

Since her death in 1886, many literary scholars have puzzled over what events might have driven her to become an invisible wraith, holed up with pen and paper. The most popular explanation is a failed romance with a mystery man, now believed to have been Reverend Charles Wadsworth, a married man she met in 1855 during one of her few outings in Philadelphia. Her letters include several fervent and openly erotic missives addressed to "Master" from "Daisy," an infantilized, victim-like "culprit" persona with a "smaller life" that she took on in these exchanges. No real agreement has ever come about the veracity of the "Master" letters, as they may have been an instance of what she stated to Higginson in discussing her poetry: "When I state myself, as the Representative of the Verse—it does not mean—me—but a supposed person."

Dickinson's and Higginson's literary relationship began when Emily read his article, "A Letter to a Young Contributor," in his magazine, and wrote, submitting her poems, asking if they were "alive" and if she could be his "scholar." Higginson did indeed find her poetry to be living, perhaps overly so, suggesting she tone down her whimsical language and meter. But he was intrigued enough to travel to Amherst in 1870. She made an exception to her general rule and agreed to meet him in person.

Dickinson, despite her lack of exposure to the world at large, had her ambitions. She read deeply the writings of women writers from which she drew inspiration—in particular George Eliot and Elizabeth Barrett Browning, going so far as to display their images—and kept up with new writers with whom she identified; the Brontë sisters' explosively passionate novels were special favorites of hers. Dickinson also studied the Bible and the new Transcendentalism, upon which she based her own female- and nature-centered theology, describing the hills of Amherst as "strong Madonnas" and herself, the Poet as "The Wayward Nun—beneath the Hill—Whose Service is to You."

Five years before Emily Dickinson passed away, a young woman, Mabel Loomis Todd, wrote a letter to her family of "the character of Amherst . . . a lady whom the people call the 'Myth'; she has not been outside of her own house in fifteen years. . . . She dresses wholly in white, and her mind is said to be perfectly wonderful." The poet had indeed captured Todd's imagination. In 1890, Todd published a volume of Emily Dickinson's poetry, a selection of her 1776 divine and abstruse poems that Emily had sewn into little booklets and tucked into a bureau.

Readers still thrill to the force of Dickinson's writing and her capacity to evoke the delicate beauty of a bee or a berry with the same scope and breadth of vision that address the big issues of God and the cosmos and sweeping emotions. The "little housekeeping person," as she described herself was in fact one of the greatest poets of all time.

Rearrange a "Wife's" affection!
When they dislocate my Brain!
Amputate my freckled Bosom!
Make me bearded like a man!

Emily Dickinson, from poem #1737

§ CHARLOTTE PERKINS GILMAN
her land is your land

Niece of Catherine Beecher and Harriet Beecher Stowe, Charlotte Perkins Gilman also felt, in her own words, "the Beecher urge to social service, the Beecher wit and gift of words." Born in 1860, Charlotte attended the Rhode Island School of Design and worked after graduation as a commercial artist.

Exposed to the "domestic feminism" of the Beechers, the extremely sensitive and imaginative young woman had resolved to avoid her mother's fate of penniless desertion by her father and assiduously avoided marriage. But after two years of relentless wooing by artist Charles W. Stetson, Charlotte reluctantly agreed to marry. After she bore her daughter Katherine, she had the nervous breakdown that inspired her famous short story, "The Yellow Wallpaper" and subsequent nonfiction accounts of her struggle with manic-depressive episodes. She wrote "The Yellow Wallpaper" for humanistic reasons: "It was not intended to drive people crazy," she said, "but to save people from being driven crazy, and it worked." Attributing her emotional problems in part to women's status in marriage, she divorced her husband and moved to California with her daughter (later, when Walter remarried, she sent Katherine to live with her father and stepmother, a move that was considered incredibly scandalous).

Although she suffered weakness and "extreme distress, shame, discouragement, and misery" her whole life, Charlotte's accomplishments are more than those of most healthy folks. A social reformer who wrote in order to push for equality for women, she lectured, founded the Women's Peace Party with Jane Addams in World War I, and wrote her best-known book, *Women and Economics,* in only seventeen days. At one point, she undertook a well-publicized debate in the *New York Times* with Anna Howard Shaw, defending her contention that women are not "rewarded in proportion to their work" as "unpaid servant(s), merely a comfort and a luxury agreeable to have if a man can afford it." Gilman was unbelievably forward-thinking for her time, even going so far as to devise architectural plans for houses without kitchens to end women's slavery to the stove so that they could take up professional occupations.

She wrote five more books pushing for economic change for women, a critically acclaimed autobiography, three utopian novels, and countless articles, stories, and poetry before her death by suicide after a long struggle with cancer in 1935.

With the passing of time, Charlotte Perkins Gilman is usually remembered only for "The Yellow Wallpaper" and for her feminist utopian novel *Herland,* in which three American men enter Herland, an all-female society that reproduces through parthenogenesis, the development of an unfertilized egg.

> *I knew it was normal and right in general, and held that a woman should be able to have marriage and motherhood, and do her work in the world, also.*
>
> Charlotte Perkins Gilman

---

§ SIMONE WEIL *the saint of all outsiders*

Complicated and committed, Simone Weil wrote with genius, though the factory and fieldwork she felt morally driven to do hurt and scarred her hands. She was born in Paris to a wealthy and loving Jewish family in 1909 and was educated in the finest schools in France.

86   Precocious politically, at ten years old she announced to her

solidly bourgeoisie family her allegiance with the Bolsheviks and began studying the party's publications. As a teen, she showed her talent for analytical thinking and wrote extensively, albeit critically, on Marxism. She described her resistance to capitalism as coming from a social consciousness that was informed by a deep understanding of the inherent elitism, imbalance of resources, and fundamental systemic flaws "between those who have the machine at their disposal and those who are at the disposal of the machine."

At the Sorbonne, her university classmates regarded Weil as brilliant but eccentric. They nicknamed her the "Red Virgin" because of the open vow of permanent chastity she made at puberty. She had also sworn to teach free classes to rail workers, farmers, and miners and had done so as an undergraduate. In later life, Weil continued to be unswervingly dedicated to the welfare and conditions of these laborers, gave most of her tiny teaching salary to them, and participated in their strikes and issues. She also worked alongside them at times as a field hand or unskilled industrial laborer.

At university, Weil majored in philosophy and was so academically gifted that she received the top certificate for "General Philosophy and Logic" after testing above classmate Simone de Beauvoir (who came in second) and all the men in the class. In *Memoirs of a Dutiful Daughter,* de Beauvoir describes Weil in a gray coverall, pockets overflowing with manifestos, surrounded by a flock of hangers-on: "She intrigued me because of her great reputation for intelligence and her bizarre get-up. Great famine had broken out in China, and I was told that when she heard the news she had wept: these tears compelled my respect much more than her gifts as a philosopher. I envied her having a heart that could beat right across the world. I managed to get near her one day. I don't know how the conversation got started; she declared in no uncertain tones that only one thing mattered in the world; the revolution which would feed all the starving people of the earth. I retorted, no less peremptorily, that the problem was not to make men happy, but to find the reason for their existence. She looked me up and down: 'It is easy to see you've never been hungry,' she snapped."

Upon graduation from the Sorbonne, Simone Weil taught high school in Le Puy for one disastrous year. Shortly after she obtained the position, Weil organized a march with the Le Puy's unemployed. Her teaching style was nontraditional, and her students couldn't pass standard midterms, but they stood loyally behind their teacher when she refused to obey her forced resignation for political activism. She greeted her firing as an occasion of gratitude and regarded it as a compliment. Her later teaching stint at Roanne went much the same way, with the exception that Anne Reynaud-Guerithault, Weil's student, had the foresight to keep her class notes. Decades later, these lectures are basic texts in philosophy courses.

Weil walked away from teaching to work as an unskilled laborer doing piecework in a factory. She couldn't keep up and barely scraped by, unable to cover her rent and food and insisting on paying her middle-class parents for every meal. Weil continued to write and also to read and study extensively both Eastern and Western traditions. She began to endure severe migraines and wrote about her spiritual yearnings.

In 1937, she traveled to Spain to aid the anarchists in the Spanish Civil War. A miserable marksman, she nevertheless was at the front lines wielding a gun; she barely missed being massacred along with her unit. She stumbled into the cooking pit and accidentally stepped in hot oil. In 1938, she began writing about her visions, a series of profound mystical experiences that moved her powerfully and were published as her spiritual autobiography.

Simone Weil and her family immigrated to America in 1942 to escape Hitler's regime, but she suffered enormous guilt and joined the Free French resistance in England. Her religious and philosophical treatises on the subject of the true nature of freedom and man's responsibly to his fellow man were regarded as a threat to the Third Reich. Though she was Jewish, she felt a great affinity for Catholicism and came to see suffering as a way to unite with God. In a letter, Weil remarked, "Every time I think of the crucifixion of Christ I commit the sin of envy."

Her moral principles would not allow her to eat more than the rations allowed in France during Nazi occupation. Malnourished, Weil fell seriously ill and contracted tuberculosis in England. Stubbornly, she maintained her self-imposed vow of deprivation and spent her last year writing some of her primary essays. On her deathbed, she wrote "The Need for Roots," in which she outlined a book she believed could serve as the foundation stone for Europe's renaissance of justice and liberty.

Simone Weil's *Waiting for God* has become one of the best-loved spiritual writings of our age. Upon her early death at age thirty-four (deemed by some to be suicide by starvation), Weil left behind a new basis for reason and some of the most exquisitely enigmatic religious thought written by anyone of any age or faith. Other great writers and thinkers fall all over themselves in her praise. Albert Camus named Simone Weil the only great spirit of our time. Andre Gide ordained her the saint of all outsiders. Flannery O'Connor called Weil a mystery that should keep us all humbled, and T. S. Eliot believed she held a kind of genius akin to that of the saints.

> *A work of art has an author and yet, when it is perfect, it has something which is essentially anonymous about it.*

Women who love
books too much

§ ZELDA SAYRE FITZGERALD *an unrealized talent*

Zelda Fitzgerald went straight from the quiet streets of Montgomery, Alabama, to the front page of the *New York Times* style section. Alongside her equally glittering husband, F. Scott Fitzgerald, she was like a shooting star heralding the initiation of a new age between the two world wars by living the fantasy life dreamed of by millions. And like a shooting star, she shone brightly with spectacular, even breathtaking appeal, and then burned out—literally. Zelda died at the age of forty-eight in a fire at a mental institution after a twenty-year battle with her inner demons.

Named by her mother after a gypsy queen in a novel she had read, Zelda seemed destined for glamour from the beginning. Stories of her antics circulated through Montgomery for decades. Like the time young Zelda got bored on a Saturday afternoon and called the fire department to alert them to a poor young girl trapped on a rooftop, and then proceeded to climb up onto her roof, kick the ladder down, and wait in glee for rescue. Or the April Fools' Day prank in which she convinced the entire senior class to take the day off. From the time she was born, she seemed always in a rush to get somewhere she could never quite reach.

90   Always referred to as a rare golden-haired beauty, much of her

magnetic attraction came from the unpredictable strength of her intensity—the sense that she could, and would, do anything at any moment. After Zelda married Scott, whose first novel *This Side of Paradise* had appeared to much acclaim, they were off on a wild ride of transatlantic partying that would capture the imagination of the entire country. From the Riviera to New York, back to Paris, and on to Washington, they always stayed at the best hotels, surrounded by society's most glamorous people, living out images from Scott's novels.

Zelda became the glamorous "First Flapper" of the Jazz Age, an era her husband had named and described as "a new generation grown up to find all gods dead, all wars fought, all faiths in man shaken." Hidden behind the glittering front-page parade, however, was a writer talented in her own right (brilliant but undisciplined, according to her husband). More tragic were the buried seeds of mental illness that began to emerge as early as 1925 when she collapsed while in Paris, leading her to began a series of prolonged treatments. In between the parties and the emotional breakdowns, she managed to write a novel called *Save Me the Waltz,* which critics believe demonstrated her great promise.

By 1930, the shooting star that was Zelda's life had sputtered into darkness. Her seclusion in a series of mental institutions was broken up by brief periods when she would return to her family filled with her legendary passion for life. Sadly, it is believed that had she lived in the present day of medical miracles her terrible bouts and sensitive emotional condition could have been treated with simple medication, and her literary prowess might have come to fruition.

> *It is very difficult to be two simple people at once,*
> *one who wants to have a law to itself and the other*

> *who wants to keep all the nice old things and be*
> *loved and safe and protected.*

Zelda Fitzgerald

──────────────

§ KATHLEEN RAINE *modern mystic*

Kathleen Raine chose the path of the visionary poet in the tradition of William Blake. Her aim was "to see World in a Grain of Sand . . . Hold Infinity in the palm of your hand," in Blake's words. She was deeply committed to this life choice and devoted enormous energy to her poetry and her essays in support of her sacred craft. She has garnered a place for herself in the pantheon of scholars of mystical poetry, with fourteen volumes of her criticism published, along with four volumes on William Blake alone and a definitive analysis of Golden Dawn idealist poet William Butler Yeats.

Born in London in 1908 and schooled at Girten College, Cambridge, Kathleen Raine undertook her master's studies in the field of natural science, using the wild landscape of her youth to inform her poetry and receiving a degree in 1929. She was the youngest and only woman among the Cambridge Poets of the 1930s and began to include women's writing as one of her interests when she read Virginia Woolf's *A Room of One's Own.*

Like some of her Romantic predecessors, she had numerous loves and married several times. Unlike others, however, her brilliance has been recognized in her lifetime; Raine received many awards for her poetry, her translations—most memorable of Honore de Balzac— and her critical work. Her verse was greatly admired by her peers, described by esteemed poet-critic G. S. Fraser as "the poems of a sibyl, perhaps of a rapt visionary, but not of a saint."

Awards notwithstanding, she was given to the occasional extreme. At one time, she refused to include any poems containing "mere human emotion." She explained this shocking and extremely limiting measure for her *Collected Poems* as a commitment to "the symbolic language of . . . poets of the 'Romantic' tradition." Her editor and publisher convinced her not to exclude some of her finest works from the ultimate volume of her verse, but her attempt to do so certainly illustrates her radical pledge to uphold her alliance to her mystic roots: "I began as a poet of spontaneous inspirations, drawing greatly on nature and fortified by my more precise biological studies. . . . I have much sympathy for the young generation now reacting against material culture. . . . I am too firmly rooted in the civilization of the past to speak their language."

> *This too is an experience of the soul. The dismembered world that once was the whole god whose broken fragments now lie dead. This passing of reality itself is real.*
>
> Kathleen Raine, from *Isis Wanderer*

§ fLANNERY O'CONNOR *literature's odd bird*

Certainly one of the most original writers in any language is Flannery O'Connor, who was born in Georgia in 1925. Her stories are all powerfully crafted, and, to the vast majority of her readers, incredibly weird. For example, Hazel Motes, backwoods protagonist

93

of her first novel *Wise Blood,* was such an ardent Christian he founded the Church of Jesus Christ without Christ and blinded himself so he could see.

Gifted with an extraordinary ear for language and an ability to evoke an almost tactile experience of the scenes she describes, Flannery O'Connor was also the odd woman out. Uninterested for the most part in the civil rights movement of her time and a devout Roman Catholic in the heart of the Fundamentalist South, she wrote stories that all—in one way or another—centered around the profoundly spiritual issue of redemption. But redemption was not a simple concept for her; it was a deeply individual evolution. And to the shock of many a good Christian, her work was populated with the bizarre, the grotesque, the maimed, and the seriously disturbed, which Flannery managed to imbue with a powerful, if twisted, sense of dignity. In a way, she was the true chronicler of the underside of Southern life, and she used her characters' physical, moral, and mental disabilities to mirror their spiritual struggles.

The most formative event of her childhood was the slow, agonizing death of her father when she was just twelve. He died of lupus—the same disease that would soon take over her own life. Literary acclaim came early. After graduating from the Georgia College for Women, she joined the Iowa Writers' Workshop, where she won the Rinehart-Iowa prize for the beginnings of *Wise Blood.* The award also gave the publisher Holt-Rinehart an option on her novel. But when Flannery turned in the early portions of *Wise Blood* to the Holt editor assigned to her, he found the manuscript "bizarre" and sent a letter offering to work with her to "change the direction" of her work into more a conventional form. Then only twenty-three years old, she politely refused and pulled the book

Another woman writer who ignored all the advice she got from men was Ellen Glasgow. In her autobiography, *The Woman Within*, she tells of the "help" she once received: "In the end, as in the beginning, Mr. Collier (a noted figure on the American literary scene) gave me no encouragement. 'The best advice I can give you,' he said, with charming candor, 'is to stop writing, and go back to the South and have some babies. . . . The greatest woman is not the woman who has written the finest book, but the woman who has had the finest babies.'" Fortunately, Ellen Glasgow, born in 1873 in Richmond, Virginia, and deaf by the time she was twenty, ignored Collier's advice. Instead she became a prolific writer, winning the Pulitzer Prize in 1942 for her novel, *In This Our Life.*

from Holt; the editor complained that she suffered from "hardening of the arteries of cooperative sense."

Flannery's vision and style were intensely personal, and though often criticized and generally misunderstood, she never wavered. She once reflected that "I have found . . . that my subject in fiction is the action of grace in territory held largely by the devil. I have also found that what I write is read by an audience which puts little stock either in grace or the devil."

After she was diagnosed with lupus in 1950, at the age of twenty-five, she moved in with her mother on a dairy farm in north Georgia. By this time lupus was controllable with massive doses of steroids, but it was a debilitating and exhausting existence. Flannery's deep religious beliefs served her well. She graciously accepted her condition and focused all the energy she had on three hours of writing each morning and raising peacocks.

When she died in 1964 at age thirty-nine, she left behind a modest body of work, including the novels *Wise Blood* (1955) and *The Violent Bear It Away* (1960), and collections of stories, *A Good Man Is Hard to Find* (1955) and *Everything That Rises Must Converge* (1965, published posthumously). But the impact of her words was never measured in quantity. She died recognized throughout the world as one of the truly great contemporary American writers.

> *I divide people into two classes: the Irksome and the Non-Irksome without regard to sex. Yes and there are the Medium Irksome and the Rare Irksome.*

Flannery O'Connor

four

Banned, Blacklisted, and Arrested

Daring Dissidents

WRITERS TURNED radicals and renegades, the women featured here were not just inspired; they were inflamed by their own activist muses. This is an especially gutsy group, both brilliant and brave, whose incendiary books got them in the hottest water, outcasts who paid the price and were usually, posthumously, embraced as leaders. Here we have the lesbian novelists who chose jail over the closet, political idealists whose unrelenting stance for their often just causes cost them their livelihood, and pioneering women who refused to be held back by gender, scandalizing society and husbands alike.

Imagine the price Anna Akhmatova paid for her refusal to go along with the pressure of the Communist Party during the purges—left with no food, no heat, her husband executed and her son jailed in the long, hard Russian winters. Never once did she give in, though, and her poetry was crystallized by hardship and grief into diamondlike perfection. Consider the shock of novelist Radclyffe Hall, once lauded and awarded for her writing, then put on trial for her gender-bending opus. Consider how it must have felt to go from critical darling to unpublishable pariah. Ponder the pressure to rat out and cave in that playwright Lillian Hellman and Algonquin Roundtable wit Dorothy Parker endured during the McCarthy scare, only to find themselves blacklisted out of a living.

Poetry ennobles the heart and eyes, and unveils the meaning of all things upon which the heart and eyes dwell. It discovers the secret rays of the universe, and restores us to forgotten paradise.

Dame Edith Sitwell

Though their books were banned and their reputations blackened, these viragos rose like so many phoenixes from the ashes of their burned books and have regained all that was lost to them, though usually not during their own lifetimes. Nadine Gordimer, the great anti-apartheid novelist, has been one of the exceptions—she received a Nobel Prize and witnessed a sea change in her native South African government that went from trying to oust and exile her to prizing her as their greatest writer. Stalwart warriors of the written word, it is to these women that we, as readers and writers, owe the most gratitude.

§ SAPPHO *the literati of Lesbos*

Lyric poet Sappho is universally regarded as the greatest ancient poet. She came to be known as the "tenth muse." Although scholars can't agree whether Homer even existed, Sappho's work was recorded and preserved by other writers. An unfortunate destruction of a volume of all her work—nine books of lyric poetry and one of elegiac verse—occurred in the early Middle Ages, engendering a search for her writing that continues even now. The Catholic Church deemed her work to be far too erotic and obscene, so they burned the volume containing her complete body of work, thus erasing what could only be some of the finest poetry in all of herstory.

Known for her powerful phrasing and intensity of feeling, erotic and otherwise, Sappho's poetry is immediate and accessible to the reader. Upon reading Sappho, you can feel that you know her, her ecstatic highs as well as the depth of her pain and longings.

Sappho is believed to have been married to a wealthy man from the island of Andros, and she had one daughter. She taught at a small college for girls who were devotees of music and poetry and, it is thought, Aphrodite. One haiku-like fragment reports that she "taught poetry to Hero, a girl athlete from the island of Gyra." She was banished to Sicily for some time, but the majority of her life was lived on the island of Lesbos. Much of her work, her most lustful in fact, is written to other women, whom she exalts for their beauty, often achieving a poetic frenzy of desire. She also writes for

SAPPHO
The tenth muse.

101

her brother Charaxus and makes the occasional reference to the political arena of the ancient world she inhabited.

Legend has it that she flung herself to her death into the sea on being rejected by the beautiful youth Phaon. This event, real or not, has been the subject of several subsequent works, including a section of Ovid's *Heroides* to plays by John Lyly in 1584 and Percy MacKaye in 1907.

> *To Atthis*
> *Though in Sardis now,*
> *she thinks of us constantly*
>
> *and of the life we shared.*
> *She saw you as a goddess*
> *and above all your dancing gave her deep joy.*
>
> *Now she shines among Lydian women like*
> *the rose fingered moon*
> *rising after sundown, erasing all*
>
> *stars around her, and pouring light equally*
> *across the salt sea*
> *and over densely flowered fields*
>
> *lucent under dew. Her light spreads*
> *on roses and tender thyme*
> *and the blooming honey-lotus*
>
> *Often while she wanders she remembers you,*
> *gentle Atthis,*
> *and desire eats away at her heart*
> *for us to come.*

§ MADAME ANNE LOUISE GERMAINE DE STAËL *Napoleonic nemesis*

You know you have really been banned when the self-appointed ruler of the world exiles you! Germaine de Staël was a noblewoman of French-Swiss decent who took full advantage of the educational opportunities her upbringing afforded her. Her father was Jacques Necker, a banker and general manager of the finances of the French monarchy and minister to Louis XVI. Her mother was Suzanne Curchod, who prior to her marriage to De Necker, was engaged to Edward Gibbon, author of the epic history, *The Decline and Fall of the Roman Empire.* The Neckers were very freethinking for their day, hosting salons and encouraging their daughter, born in 1766—ten years before the revolution in America—to read and write, and to form her own opinions. Germaine certainly made good on that, becoming the foremost female intellectual of the Romantic period.

In 1786, she married the baron de Staël-Holstein, ambassador of Sweden. Their marriage was tumultuous and she took many lovers, most notably the

GERMAINE DE STAËL *Liberated even before France.*

Romantic poet August Schlegel and Benjamin Constant, a writer with liberation politics who became her longtime companion. In Paris, Madame de Staël formed a salon, a hotbed of politics and culture. She invited new and established writers, artists, and thinkers alike.

Her praise of the German State prompted Napoleon to banish her from France. She picked up her life and moved to an estate she maintained in Switzerland at Coppet on Lake Geneva, where she assembled another and equally dazzling group of cerebral companions, including Jean-Jacques Rousseau, Lord Byron, and Percy Bysshe Shelly.

As a writer, de Staël greatly influenced the Europe of the day with her cardinal work *On Germany,* as well as her novels *Delphine* and *Corinne of Italy,* a nonfiction sociological study of literature, and her memoir, *Ten Years of Exile,* published in 1818.

Corinne is her best-loved work, a daring story of an affair between a brilliant Italian woman and an English noble that explores themes of purity, free love, the place of domesticity, Italian art, architecture, geography, politics, and woman as genius as seen though the Romantic lens. Even today, Madame de Staël has not quite escaped her banned status. At this writing there is no English translation of *Corinne* in print, and prior to the most recent one, there had been no new translation of the novel in nearly 100 years, despite de Staël's status as one of the preeminent women of letters of all time.

> *Wit consists in knowing the resemblance of things
> which differ and the difference of things which are
> alike.*
>
> Madame de Staël

§ HARRIET BEECHER STOWE *civil warrior*

Most schoolchildren are taught that Harriet Beecher Stowe was an extremely creative young woman who, almost accidentally, wrote a book that tore America apart. The truth is that *Uncle Tom's Cabin* was written with precisely the intent to publicize the cruelty of slavery and to galvanize people to act. It came as no surprise when her book was banned in the South as subversive. (It still makes lists of banned books today.)

Extremely bright, even as a child Harriet was keenly interested in improving humanity. Born in 1811, she lived a large family of nine children. Her father was a Calvinist minister; her mother died when she was five. She was very attached to her older sister, Catherine, who founded the Hartford Female Seminary. The year 1832 found the Beecher family leaving their longtime home of Litchfield, Connecticut, and moving to Cincinnati, right across the Ohio River from Kentucky. From this vantage point so much closer to the South, Harriet had much greater exposure to slavery. A young, idealistic student of theology, Harriet was horrified. Her brothers became involved in the antislavery movement and were extremely vocal about their feelings. Harriet, for her part, aided a runaway slave.

HARRIET BEECHER STOWE *The "little lady who made this big war," according to Abe Lincoln.*

In 1836, Harriet met Calvin Stowe, one of the professors of religion at her father's seminary, married him, and eventually bore six children. Around this time, she discovered her love of writing, contributing articles to numerous religious magazines and papers. She also began working on her first novel, *The Mayflower: Sketches and Scenes and Characters among the Descendants of the Puritans.*

In 1850, the Fugitive Slave Acts passed Congress. It was this event that moved Harriet to write *Uncle Tom's Cabin.* She couldn't abide the inhumanity of slaves being hunted down and forcibly returned to their former owners after struggling so hard for the freedom that was their birthright. Horror stories of the torture of runaway slaves galvanized the sensitive Harriet to action, and she wrote the book with the full intention of sending out a cry against the whippings, maimings, and hangings of slaves.

Uncle Tom's Cabin or Live Among the Lonely was first run as a series of installments in the national *Era,* an abolitionist newspaper. Upon publication in book form in 1852, Stowe's work was very well received. The entire printing of 5,000 copies sold out in two days and 3 million copies of the book were sold around the world before the advent of the Civil War! Harriet had outstripped her wildest dreams and had truly fired the first shot in what was to become the War between the States. She also received critical acclaim from such literary luminaries as Henry Wadsworth Longfellow and Leo Tolstoy, who declared *Uncle Tom's Cabin* the "highest moral art." Abraham Lincoln himself called Harriet "the little lady who made this big war."

Harriet's strategy was to show the extremes of slavery, culminating in the savage beating of the gentle old slave, Tom. The world was captivated by Stowe's dramatic story. Reviled in the South, Stowe met all her pro-slave detractors with dignity, even going so far as to publish a critical *Key to Uncle Tom's Cabin* and write a second novel about the plight of slaves in *Dred: A Tale of the Great Dismal Swamp.*

Basking in her fame, she and her husband traveled in Europe, where she was lauded everywhere she went. In the 1860s, she wrote a series of books on her husband's recollections of his childhood in New England. These are considered to be some of the first of what came to be called "local color writing" in New England.

> *I won't be any properer than I have a mind to be.*

> Harriet Beecher Stowe

§ ANGELINA EMILY AND SARAH MOORE GRIMKÉ *forces to be reckoned with*

The Grimké sisters were raised in the South in the early 1800s, like Scarlett and her sisters in *Gone with the Wind,* but unlike the fictional characters, the sisters grew up hating slavery. The privileged duo, two of twelve children, had all the Southern advantages of private tutors and training in the arts at their palatial Charleston, South Carolina, home and were brought up to be good, high-church Episcopalians. But they first showed their abolitionist spunk when Sarah was twelve; she was caught teaching a slave to read and write, a criminal offense. Because Angelina supported her, they both were punished.

As soon as they could, they left the South. Sarah moved to Philadelphia in 1821 and converted to Quakerism because of its antislavery beliefs. Angelina followed eight years later.

A fervent abolitionist writer, Angelina had a nose for publicity and got her passionate condemnation of slavery published in William Lloyd Garrison's magazine, the *Liberator*. She followed this up with a pamphlet entitled "An Appeal to the Christian Women of the South," which tried to appeal to women's consciences in opposing slavery: "But, perhaps you will be ready to query, why appeal to women on this subject? We do not make the law which perpetuates slavery. No legislative power is vested in us; we can do nothing to overthrow the system, even if we wished to do so. To this I reply, I know you do not make the laws, but I also know that you are the wives and mothers, the sisters and daughters of those who do; and if you really suppose you can do nothing to overthrow slavery, you are greatly mistaken. . . . 1st. You can read on this subject. 2nd. You can pray over this subject. 3rd. You can speak on this subject. 4th. You can act on this subject."

Her appeal created a storm of controversy. In her hometown of

Charleston, the postmaster burned all copies and put out a warning that Angelina had better never return to the South. At that point, sister Sarah took up the charge and attacked the religious defense of slavery in her "Epistle to the Clergy of the Southern States."

The fearless siblings took their abolitionist act on the road, speaking to mixed crowds of men and women. This raised the hackles of so-called "proper" society—ladies were not supposed to appear in public with men who were not their husbands, and women were not supposed to lecture or preach—who returned fire with a printed attack from the Massachusetts' clergy that was preached to every available congregation in 1837. In it, the clergy condemned women reformers and preachers, issuing a caution regarding any female who "assumed the place and tone of man as public reformer. . . . Her character becomes unnatural."

The irrepressible duo fired back in grand style with letters in the *Spectator* and in Sarah's book, published in 1838, *Letters on the Equality of the Sexes and the Condition of Women.* This was a brilliant manifesto declaring women as absolutely and naturally endowed with equal rights, and that the only "unnatural" behaviors being performed in American society were those of men suppressing women. Later, Angelina became the first woman in America to speak to a legislature when she presented her antislavery petition, signed by 20,000 women, to the Massachusetts state legislative body.

The duo fought against slavery and for women's rights their whole lives. They even caught the eye of Henry David Thoreau, who described them as "two elderly gray-headed ladies, the former in extreme Bloomer costume, which was what you might call remarkable."

I ask for no favors for my sex. I surrender no claim to equality. All I ask our brethren is, that they will take their feet from off our necks and permit us to stand upright on the ground which God designed us to occupy.

Sarah Grimké

---

§ RADCLYFFE HALL *soldier of fortune*

Preferring tweeds to tulle, pioneering lesbian novelist Radclyffe Hall spent her life trying to find herself, but ironically she has nearly been lost to modern readers. One can only hope that a biographer as accomplished as Diane Middlebrook will rescue her, alongside Billy Tipton, from the dustbin of history. What we do know about Hall from Lady Una Troubridge, her lover for more than a quarter-century, is that she was born in 1886 in Bournemouth, Hampshire, and had a wretched childhood. Abandoned by her father by age three and ignored by a mother preoccupied with a romance, Marguerite Radclyffe Hall began her life with a sense that she didn't matter. This was greatly reinforced when Mrs. Hall remarried an Italian singing instructor who matched both mother and father in his cruel inattention to the growing girl.

By her teens, Radclyffe was alternately calling herself Peter or John and had one relatively unsuccessful year at King's College during which she struggled with her sexuality. At the age viewed as adulthood by most, twenty-one, Radclyffe inherited an immense trust fund and tried to forge a new life with her only familial tie, her mother's mother, with whom she moved to Kensington. Hall's grandmother had been the only source of affection up to that point. This relationship seems to have set a pattern for her future, as her first serious romance was with a woman twenty-three years her senior. The older woman, Mabel Veronica Batten, was a music patron with a secure position in society. She mentored Radclyffe and urged her to give up sports and take up more acceptable pursuits such as books and horses. Mabel Batten provided Hall with the education and nurturing she had missed in her childhood and molded her into an intellectual seeker and writer. Batten died in 1916 and Una Troubridge's friendship during Hall's grief led to love. They remained partners, living together until Hall's death in 1943.

Hall dressed as a man, in beautifully cut custom tweed suits and short clipped hair, which was shocking to some gentlefolk. A serious writer, Hall published several books of poetry and two novels before winning public attention in 1926, when she won the Femina-Vie Heureuse Prize and the James Tait Black Memorial Book Prize for *Adam's Breed*, a novel of religious awakening.

Her writerly accomplishments didn't garner her nearly the attention she received for the commotion about her 1928 novel *The Well of Loneliness,* the depiction of a troubled but full and unclos-eted pursuit of happiness. With an introduction written by no less an authority than psychologist Havelock Ellis, Hall told the story of a girl named Stephen Gordon whose father wanted a son, not the daughter born to him. Stephen is a lively protagonist, pursuing other women lustily and working with the London Ambulance Column during World War I. Stephen professes to be a man inside a woman's body, trying to deal with the difficulties of the congenital invert in this portrayal of the lesbian as a biological blight.

Problematic for the more psychoanalyzed and feminized reader of today, *The Well of Loneliness* was extremely radical for 1928. It exploded like one of the WWI shells that wounded Stephen's ambulance passengers. The scandal following Hall's new book concluded with a trial and the book's prohibition. Several notables such as Virginia Woolf and Vera Brittain rushed to her defense, but English courts banned the book. Just like the subjugation of sapphists, both Stephen Gordon, the character, and her creator, Radclyffe Hall, were squelched. Radclyffe Hall followed her banned opus with several religious fictions, but the prosecution caused her to limit the scope of her subject matter, and sadly, she was largely ignored from then on.

> *The coming of war had completely altered the complexion of her life, at all events for three years.*
>
> Radclyffe Hall, from *Miss Ogilvy Finds Herself*

§ ANNA AKHMATOVA *brilliance unbowed*

A poet and writer of the highest personal and literary standards, during her lifetime Anna Akhmatova was denied her deserved international reputation as one of Russia's greatest writers. Of noble birth, Anna Gorenko was born in Odessa, Ukraine, in 1889. Indicating the independent nature that became her hallmark, she changed her name when she was seventeen. She went on to study law at university, but always wrote poetry. During this time, she met Nikolai Gumilev, a poet and literary critic with whom she shared a love of literature. They married in 1910 and together threw themselves into Acmeism, a literary school dedicated to clear and tightly constructed verse in reaction to the ruling style of the day, Russia's popular symbolism. Gumilev, a romantic figure with distant dreams, took off for Africa, leaving his new bride on her own for great stretches of time. Focused on her poetry, Anna had her first book, *Evening,* published to high praise in 1911. A striking Tartar beauty, Akhmatova developed a great following and read to doting crowds at an underground cabaret, the Stray Dog café. That same

year, she gave birth to son Lev. Domesticity was not Anna's destiny, however, and Gumilev's mother, who despised Anna, took Lev from her.

While the couple explored their craft, chaos surrounded their home in St. Petersburg. Toward the end of the nineteenth century, Russia's tsars had been under attack politically, and parties formed illegally in opposition to the royal rulers. One such party was the Social Democratic Party, a faction of which was led by Vladimir Lenin. Lenin's sect, the Bolsheviks, were fairly radical in their fervor to effect the overthrow of the tsar, seemingly by any means.

Anna's second book, *Rosary,* debuted in 1913 to even greater fervor, so much so that the book inspired a parlor game in which each person took turns quoting a verse until the entire book was finished.

ANNA AKHMATOVA *Persecuted and starved by Stalin, she refused to stop writing.*

Anna's success caused strife at home; her husband was quite jealous, and they both began relationships outside the marriage. The two writers eventually divorced, and Anna married Voldemar Shileiko, but she and her first husband maintained a friendship. Anna suffered a severe shock when the Bolsheviks executed her first husband in 1921 over a trumped-up charge of a plot to overthrow the government. Anna's book *Anno Domini* came out the following year. She, in turn, suffered at the Bolsheviks' hands and became something of a pariah.

This was a time of great hardship when Anna's household rarely had enough to eat or fuel for heat. Most of their friends left Russia during this terrible time of persecution. By 1924, in the wake of Lenin's death, Stalin had taken power and waged even greater terror over the Russian people. During his "purges," million of people were killed and imprisoned, including any writer who didn't bow to the dictates of the new regime. Anna's son Lev was arrested in 1933 and 1935, and her writings were banned from 1925 to 1940. She turned to literary criticism and translation and Pushkin scholarship. During the 1930s, she courageously composed an epic poem, "Requiem," in honor of Stalin's victims, which went unpublished in Russian until 1987. In 1940, an anthology of her poetry, *From Six Books,* was published, only to be withdrawn a month later.

During Germany's siege of the Soviet Union in 1941, Anna urged the women of Leningrad, formerly St. Petersburg, to be brave during this war. Astoundingly the government, knowing her status as a beloved and respected figure in Russian culture, had asked her to do this even though they forbade the publication of her writing.

The postwar period found Anna enjoying popularity once again briefly, but Andrei Zhadanov, Secretary of the Central Committee, soon removed her from the Writer's Union and decreed a ban on her writing, destroying a book of her poems and decrying her as "half nun, half harlot." Expulsion also lost Anna her ration card and any means of food and supplies, forcing her to ask support from friends until the end of her life. In 1949, Lev Gumilev was arrested again and imprisoned for seven years, until Nikita Khrushchev took leadership of the party, denounced Stalin, and released prisoners.

Anna's poetry was published in the late '50s with heavy-handed censorship. Now legendary to the youth of Russia for her staunch idealism and enduring dedication to poetry, budding Russian literati including Joseph Brodsky sought her out as a connection to pre-Communist Russia. A great admirer of the great lady of letters from the "Silver Age" of Russian poetry, who survived the devastation of the Communist holocaust, Brodsky named Anna Akhmatova "the muse of keening" for her elegies for the dead and for a dying culture.

> *We thought: we're poor, we have nothing, but when*
> *we started losing one after the other*
>
> *So each day became remembrance day.*
>
> Anna Akhmatova, from *In Memoriam, July 19, 1914*

§ KATE CHOPIN *dangerous deb*

Nineteenth-century ladies were not encouraged to write frankly about sex. Anyone who did most certainly found herself in the center of a hot scandal. Kate Chopin's *The Awakening*, fiercely brave at the time and hugely controversial, was an open and honest examination of her own sexuality and her coming of age. Published in 1899, *The Awakening* was attacked as an essentially vulgar story; libraries banned the book immediately, even in her hometown of St. Louis. Chopin was refused publication of her collection of short stories shortly thereafter and experienced a sense of failure after the storm of bad press and rejection of her book. She died in 1904, having been paid only a pittance in royalties, and her brave book fell into the shadows until it was rediscovered by feminist scholars in the 1960s.

Kate Chopin came from a privileged St. Louis background as the daughter of a French Creole aristocrat mother and a hardworking, very successful Irish immigrant father. Raised as a strict Catholic, Kate had a primly proper Victorian upbringing and emerged as a debutante and belle of the great river town. Her successful debut in St. Louis society led to a happy marriage to a wealthy New Orleans Creole cotton trader, Oscar Chopin, who bought a plantation in Cloutierville. The couple had several children, and Kate was, in all ways, a dutiful and devoted wife and mother who always kept journals and diaries.

Throughout history, reading was often seen as corrupting to women. Many men believed that women should not be taught to read unless "they wish to be nuns," writes the nobleman Philippe de Novare in the fifteenth century, "since they might otherwise, coming of age, write or receive amorous missives."

The loss of her husband to swamp fever in 1883 devastated Kate Chopin. During her mourning period, she went beyond her self-described "scribbles" and started writing seriously. The bereaved family returned to St. Louis and set about creating a new life. Critics received Kate's stories as charming portraits of "genteel Creole life." (But the same set of reviewers who lauded the storyteller turned savage when Chopin presented *The Awakening*.)

After settling back in her hometown, Kate Chopin was befriended by her family physician, Dr. Frederick Kolbenheyer. A voracious reader who eschewed religion, he directed Kate to read Aldous Huxley, Charles Darwin, Gustave Flaubert, Sarah Orne Jewett, Emile Zola, and Mary Wilkins Freeman.

One recommended writer particularly struck a cord with Kate: Guy de Maupassant. The Frenchman's espousal of liberty and his disregard for literary convention greatly inspired her. This pursuit for freedom came across clearly in *The Awakening*'s central female character, Edna Pontellier. This is obvious in Edna's choice about her way of life and demand for equality in the boudoir, "I give myself where I please."

The critics who preferred corsets laced up tightly and women in their place dashed Kate Chopin's daring. Their burial of her book for more than fifty years was an enormous loss to American readers. Shortly after its "rediscovery" in the 1960s, the novel was hailed as a classic and a feminist breakthrough. Scholars poring over the body of Chopin's work have gone on to identify the elegant subversiveness in her early stories. There has been speculation that the shame and discredit over her novel caused her illness and death, but the blow she struck for women's erotic liberation still reverberates nearly a century later.

> When she abandoned herself a little whispered word escaped her slightly parted lips. She said it over and over under her breath; free, free, free!

Kate Chopin, from "The Going Away of Liza"

§ MERIDEL LE SUEUR *prairie populist*

Perhaps it was Meridel Le Sueur's birth at the turn of the twentieth century that marked her for a forward-thinking life filled with dreams of a better tomorrow. A native of Murray, Iowa, in America's heartland, Meridel and her stepfather-guardian (Mama and Papa were long gone) made their way south, living in Kansas, Oklahoma, and Texas. Her childhood was fairly unusual; her stepfather was a virulent Socialist and the women he exposed Meridel to were fellow radicals. Her lifelong idealism was ingrained at an early age and she lived a much freer life than most women of her day. As prolific as she was opinionated, Le Sueur was taught to work for the common political cause and learned the best way she could help spread the word was by writing about it. Ultimately, she came to make her living mostly as a journalist and biographer, receiving good notices for her short stories, poetry, and novels, as well.

Le Sueur's life and work were one and the same. She lived in an anarchist commune for a time with none other than the fiery radical Emma Goldman. She and her like-minded associates were strenuously advocating for a redistribution of wealth to American laborers and the poor. As a journalist, Le Sueur was firmly entrenched in the leftmost political viewpoint; her bibliography includes *Anvil, Daily Worker, Dial, New Masses, Pagany, Partisan Review,* and *Scribner's.* Her gypsy childhood made for a sense of adventure, and she also acted in early Hollywood and did a stint as director of the Little Theater in Sacramento, California.

Le Sueur never gave up her writing, though, and turned to recording the stories of plain folk in her social history, *North Star Country.* This endeavor attracted much attention for its use of the common parlance and faithful ear to oral source material. She married a labor organizer, Harry Rice, and raised a family. In 1928, Le Sueur had the first of two daughters and began to think of her daughter's life ahead of her. Her early stories of America's ordinary townspeople and farmers evolved into studies of working class and pioneer women and the solidarity between them.

The McCarthy era was not good to Meridel; she was blacklisted as a Communist sympathizer. The blacklisting led to critical neglect of her writing even though she was just hitting her stride with her prizewinning prairie populist papers. She wrote several books that went unpublished because of her damning blacklisted status until near the end of her life.

Though she labored in obscurity, Meridel Le Sueur continued the bright positivism that marked her politics and her passions. Throughout her life, she believed a better world was inevitable and that this wonderful new future would soon be "birthed." Her book, *Ancient Rites of Ripening,* written at the age of eighty-two, bespeaks her anticipation of society's rehabilitation through the influence of women. In her later years, she also wrote books for children with an emphasis on nature and values, including *Sparrow Hawk* and the story of Abe Lincoln's mother, *Nancy Hank of Wilderness.* Ever the diligent dreamer, Meridel Le Sueur sang the song of the unsung.

> *Old men and tramps lie on the grass all day. It is hard to get work. Many people beside Karl are out of work. People are hungry just as I am hungry. People are ready to flower and they cannot.*

Meridel Le Sueur, from *Annunciation*

Dawn Powell, contemporary of Theodore Dreiser, Ernest Hemingway, and John Dos Passos, could drink them under the table and hold her own in hard living as well as in the prodigious output of novels. Her life and work have certainly taken plot twists even she might have been hard pressed to dream up, from toast of the town to scattered bag of bones.

An Ohio girl who escaped to Greenwich Village as a permanent visitor, Powell looked at Manhattan and its citizens with a comic eye. An original voice whose titles alone—*The Wicked Pavilion, The Locusts Have No King, Angels on Toast*—evince a creativity and cheek, Powell wrote fifteen slightly shocking books which quickly slid out of print and, after her death in 1965, were held hostage by a literary executrix who refused all queries until threatened with legal action.

Powell's life didn't fit the cookie-cutter mold of flag-waving World War II. A friend of Dorothy Parker, she was an inveterate writer of juicy letters and essays such as her "drinking tour" of New York City. Her open marriage to an impoverished alcoholic poet, her scarily silent savant son, and her predilection for bar fights made the satirist risque reading.

Not the best candidate for white-glove publicity, the critically regarded Powell did appeal to a small number of select sophisticates. Ernest Hemingway named her "his favorite living writer," and Gore Vidal campaigned to have her acknowledged as America's greatest comic writer.

Low sales aside, however, Dawn Powell watched her brilliant career go up in smoke and suffered intolerable indignities even after her death. She willed her body to science, only to have her corpse thrown onto a field by a day crew of convicts, her remains mixed in with a jumble of paupers, prostitutes, and orphans.

While most '40s readers might not have been ready for Dawn Powell's send-ups of New York society, a new generation is primed for her wicked and wise pen. Discovered by literary champion Tim Page, a Pulitzer Prize-winning critic for the *Washington Post*, Powell's novels are finally seeing the light of day. Page, who describes her as having "a dark, mordant attitude toward that world [that] rankled," happened upon Dawn while reading Edmund Wilson's decades-old essay declaring Powell the equal of Evelyn Waugh and Muriel Spark. For a few thousand dollars, Page bought her entire literary estate and donated it to Columbia, and is shepherding her blacklisted backlist back into print.

> *I give them their heads. They furnish their own nooses.*
>
> Dawn Powell, speaking about her characters

§ LENORE KANDEL *word alchemist*

Bold and beautiful, Lenore Kandel's poetry attempts to bridge the chasm between the sacred and the sexual, between religion and the eroticism of the body. Replete with tantric symbolism, her works reflect Buddhist influence as well as a celebration of the corporeal.

Born in New York City in 1932, Lenore moved with her family that same year to Los Angeles, when her father, the novelist Aben Kandel, got a movie deal for his novel, *City in Conquest.* A minor classic, the film starred Jimmy Cagney.

Banned, Blacklisted, and Arrested
Daring Dissidents

By the age of twelve, Lenore had decided to become a Buddhist and started writing. She spent the next fifteen years going to school and reading voraciously, "everything I could get my hands on, particularly about world religions." In 1959, she began sitting zazen in New York and had three short collections of her poetry published. In 1960, she moved to San Francisco and met Beat poet Lew Welch at East-West House, a co-op started by Gary Snyder and other Zen students.

Welch was on the scene in the early part of the San Francisco Renaissance, the collection of poetry schools in the Bay Area pulled together by Robert Duncan in his efforts to create a poetry community after the fall of Black Mountain College in North Carolina. Lew was intertwined in the mesh of the Beat and the Black Mountain College scene, but refused to align with any one school of poetry. He was friends with Jack Kerouac, Lawrence Ferlinghetti, and fellow Buddhist scholar Gary Snyder.

Lenore recalls how she ended up in San Francisco, living at the East-West House and studying with Shunryu Suzuki Roshi. "I'd been meaning to come to San Francisco, and I decided to come here for a weekend and I stayed. I met Lew and all the people in that whole trip and when Jack came into town, we all went to Big Sur."

An omnivorous reader, Lenore was very familiar with Jack Kerouac's work and was especially fond of *On the Road*. His poetic style piqued her interest, and she found him to be inspiring to her own work. He too was impressed by her intensity and intellect as well as her physical stature. It would be in Jack's *Big Sur* that he would immortalize Lenore as "a big Rumanian monster beauty of some kind I mean with big purple eyes and very tall and big (but Mae West big), but also intelligent, well read, writes poetry, is a Zen student, knows everything." She was tall, indeed taller and larger than Lew, yet she carried a distinctly female aura, and was described by Carolyn Cassady in *Off the Road* as a "Fertility Goddess."

Like many of the other Beats, her work provoked controversy. *The Love Book,* her most notorious collection of what she calls "holy erotica," sent shock waves throughout the San Francisco Bay Area when it was published in 1965. After police raids on the Psychedelic Shop and City Lights bookstore in San Francisco, the chapbook was deemed pornographic and obscene. When challenged in court, Lenore defended it as a "twenty-three-year search for an appropriate way to worship" and an attempt to "express her belief that sexual acts between loving persons are religious acts."

Although Lenore has been incapacitated since 1970 from a motorcycle accident with her then-husband, Hell's Angel William Fritsch, she still reads voraciously on all subjects, including religion, and writes daily. "It's important to be a speaker of truth, especially if you put your words out there, they gotta be true."

Kenneth Rexroth once praised the fluidity and striking austerity of her words, which he saw as delineating the sharp paradoxes of the body and soul. Disregarding convention, she delves into the essence of being, writing provocative poems that intend to stir the heart as well as the mind. The strong Buddhist influence in her work molds emotions into stanzas, giving shape to the ineffable. Lenore Kandel is a true word alchemist.

> *we have all been brothers, hermaphroditic as oysters*
> *bestowing our pearls carelessly*
> *no one yet had invented ownership*
> *nor guilt   nor time*

Lenore Kandel, from "Enlightenment Poem"

South African Nadine Gordimer's unstinting literary resistance and refusal to back down is a testimony to bravery. She dared to face powerful opposition to her writing about government-sanctioned racial oppression that normalized daily beatings, jailings, and murder. Three of her books were banned, but she never stopped exercising her right as an artist to state openly her condemnation of apartheid. Beloved by anyone who had read her fiction and hated by anyone who feared the polemic potential of her writing, this defiant woman helped created the post-apartheid future she envisioned in her novels.

She was born in 1923 in the East Rand town of Spring, to a Latvian jeweler father who had been drawn to the diamond mining money in the southern Traansvaal tip of Africa and a hypochondriac British mother. Nadine was frequently kept home from convent school by her housebound mother and, at age nine, felt the urge to pick up a pen. By the time she was fifteen, *Forum* magazine had published a story by the gifted girl.

Through her father's business she came to learn of the terrible conditions in the diamond mines. Mines managed by whites who sent black South Africans into the hot and dangerous shafts quickly taught the sensitive and observant Nadine about the striated society ordained by the white Afrikaners in power. The sense of injustice that informed her sensibility as a young woman only developed with time as the incongruity of colonial cruelty increased in a country straining toward modernity.

Gordimer claims as a major influence Georg Lukacs, a Hungarian philosopher and essayist, whose writings at the turn of the century and beyond helped shape European realism. Gordimer's first book, *The Lying Days,* was published in 1953 and traced the impact of Europeans in Africa. From this historical beginning, her short stories and novels amplified her complaint against acculturated segregation and a caste system enforced upon the people native to Africa. Reviewer Maxwell Geismar declared her fiction "a luminous symbol of at least one white person's understanding of the black man's burden."

The novels that have emerged as a legacy for the outcast writer include *The Conservationist, July's People,* and *Burger's Daughter.* Readers praise Gordimer's painterly quality of rich detail, full characterization, and symbolic setting, though a few object to the mechanics of her narratives, judging it as unfashionable to see a story through to completion. A few critics even carp at her attention to race and lack thereof to feminism, but her own insistence is to speak to the issues of humankind, inclusive of race and gender.

Decried by whites in her home country, Nadine Gordimer continued to live in Johannesburg despite pressure to leave. For a time, recognition of her skill as a writer and the validity of her message only came from abroad. The *New Yorker* published her often, and she taught in American universities during

NADINE GORDIMER *For a time, this anti-apartheid novelist was popular everywhere in the world but her native South Africa.*

the politically restive '60s and '70s. After the Soweto uprising in South Africa, her powerful novel *Burger's Daughter* was banned for its potential to inflame insurrectionists. In response, Gordimer focused with greater intent on her political opposition to apartheid and cofounded the Congress of South African Writers. She went on to work in documentary films along with her son Hugo Cassirer and published nonfiction about subjects specific to South Africa. She refused the Orange Award because of its restriction to women, but joined the exclusive ennead of Nobel-winning women in 1991. The prize was granted, in the words of the committee, because "her magnificent epic writing has—in the words of Alfred Nobel—been of very great benefit to humanity."

At great personal risk and in spite of a constant threat of ostracism, this woman's pen marked the dividing line between black and white South Africa and the ways of life on either side. With unmatched lucidity, she examined the rituals of persecution and life under the fist. Her Nobel Prize for Literature was a tribute to her singular courage and life's work of telling the truth through fiction.

> *Perhaps more than the work of any other writer, the novels of Nadine Gordimer have given imaginative and moral shape to the recent history of South Africa.*
>
> Jay Dillemuth, *The Norton Anthology of English Literature*

I was gravely warned by some of my female acquaintances that no woman could expect to be regarded as a lady after she had written a book.

Lydia M. Child

JUDY BLUME LEADS WITH FIVE

Challenged, burned, or banned books in the United States in the past fifteen years:

The Clan of the Cave Bear by Jean Auel

The Color Purple by Alice Walker

Diary of a Young Girl by Anne Frank

Flowers in the Attic by V. C. Andrews

Forever by Judy Blume

Harriet the Spy by Louise Fitzhugh

I Know Why the Caged Bird Sings
  by Maya Angelou

Iggie's House by Judy Blume

It's Okay If You Don't Love Me
  by Norma Klein

Love Is One of the Choices
  by Norma Klein

Ordinary People by Judith Guest

Silas Marner by George Eliot

Superfudge by Judy Blume

Uncle Tom's Cabin
  by Harriet Beecher Stowe

The Handmaiden's Tale
  by Margaret Atwood

Changing Bodies, Changing Lives
  by Ruth Bell

A Wrinkle in Time by Madeleine L'Engle

Beloved by Toni Morrison

The Joy Luck Club by Amy Tan

Little House in the Big Woods
  by Laura Ingalls Wilder

Bridge to Terabithia
  by Katherine Paterson

Blubber by Judy Blume

Heather Has Two Mommies
  by Lesléa Newman

The Headless Cupid by Zilpha Snyder

The Great Gilly Hopkins
  by Katherine Paterson

On My Honor by Marion Dane Bauer

My House by Nikki Giovanni

Then Again, Maybe I Won't
  by Judy Blume

My Friend Flicka by Mary O'Hara

"You're going to be famous," Billie Holiday told Maya Angelou in 1958, "but it won't be for singing." Billie was prophetic. Mute as a child, Maya Angelou has gone on to become one of the most powerful voices in American society today. Who can ever forget that powerful, precise voice that dominated the 1993 inauguration of President Bill Clinton as she recited "On the Pulse of Morning"?

Her journey from silence to worldwide acclaim is an amazing one, told by her in five autobiographical volumes: *I Know Why the Caged Bird Sings; Gather Together in My Name; Singin' and Swingin' and Gettin' Merry Like Christmas; The Heart of a Woman;* and *All God's Children Need Traveling Shoes.* But it is precisely one of these volumes, *Caged Bird,* that has garnered her the dubious distinction of being one of the most banned writers in the United States. The powerful depiction of her childhood rape has caused schools and libraries across the country to deem it "inappropriate."

Maya Angelou was born Marguerite Johnson in St. Louis in 1928. At age three she was sent to live with her paternal grandmother in Stamps, Arkansas, a town so segregated that many black children, she claimed, "didn't, really, absolutely know what whites looked like."

" 'Thou shall not be dirty' and 'Thou shall not be impudent' were the two commandments of Grandmother Henderson upon which hung our total salvation," she remembers in *I Know Why the Caged Bird Sings.* "Each night in the bitterest winter we were forced to wash faces, arms, necks, legs and feet before going to bed. She used to add, with a smirk that unprofane people can't control when venturing into profanity, 'and wash as far as possible, then wash possible.' "

From 1901 to 1999, only nine women have received this prestigious award for literature.

Selma Ottilia Lovisa Lagerlöf (1909), "in appreciation of the lofty idealism, vivid imagination, and spiritual perception that characterize her writings."

Grazia Deledda (1926), "for her idealistically inspired writings which with plastic clarity picture the life on her native island and with depth and sympathy deal with human problems in general."

Sigrid Undset (1928), "principally for her powerful descriptions of Northern life during the Middle Ages."

Pearl Buck (1938), "for her rich and truly epic descriptions of peasant life in China and for her biographical masterpieces."

Gabriela Mistral (1945), "for her lyric poetry which, inspired by powerful emotions, has made her name a symbol of the idealistic aspirations of the entire Latin American world."

Nelly Sachs (1966; shared), "for her outstanding lyrical and dramatic writing, which interprets Israel's destiny with touching strength."

Nadine Gordimer (1991) her politically charged epic writing helped end apartheid and, in the words of Alfred Nobel, have "been of a very great benefit to humanity."

Toni Morrison (1993), "who in novels characterized by visionary force and poetic import, gives life to an essential aspect of American reality."

Wislawa Szymborska (1996), "for poetry that with ironic precision allows the historical and biological context to come to light in fragments of human reality."

When she was seven, on a visit to her mother, she was raped by her mother's boyfriend. She reported this to her mother, and the man was tried and sent to jail, which confused and upset the young girl. When he was killed in prison for being a child molester, she felt responsible and spent the next five years in total silence.

With the help of her grandmother and another woman, Bertha

Flowers, who introduced her to literature, Maya slowly came out of herself, graduating at the top of her eighth-grade class, and moved to San Francisco to live in her mother's boarding house. She went to school, took dance and drama lessons, and in her spare time, became the first African American streetcar conductor in San Francisco. An unplanned pregnancy made her a mother at age sixteen, and she later had a short-lived marriage with Tosh Angelos, still later adapting his surname and taking as her first name the nickname her brother used for her.

MAYA ANGELOU *One of the most often banned writers in America for her completely honest autobiography.*

Working at a variety of odd jobs, she eventually began to make a living as a singer and dancer. In 1954, she toured Europe and Africa with a State Department-sponsored production of *Porgy and Bess*. Upon returning to the United States, she created a revue, Cabaret for Freedom, as a benefit for Martin Luther King, Jr.'s Southern Christian Leadership Conference (SCLC). Later, at King's request, she served as the northern coordinator for the SCLC.

In 1961, she left the United States with her son and her lover, Vusumzi Make, a South African freedom fighter, to live in Cairo, where she tried to become the editor of the *Arab Observer*. The Egyptians wouldn't think of a woman in the position, and her lover was equally outraged. She left him and moved to Ghana, where she lived for five years, working as an editor and writer for various newspapers and teaching at the University of Ghana. She loved the people of Ghana. "Their skins were the colors of my childhood cravings: peanut butter, licorice, chocolate, caramel. There was the laughter of home, quick and without artifice," she wrote in *All God's Children Need Traveling Shoes.* But she never felt completely accepted and returned to the United States in 1966.

She began writing books at the urging of James Baldwin, who had heard her tell her childhood stories and encouraged her to write them down. (Another story has it that it was a chance meeting with cartoonist Jules Feiffer that was the impetus.) But the multitalented dynamo continued to act in both plays and films and began to write poetry and plays as well. In 1972, she became the first African American woman to have a screenplay, *Georgia, Georgia,* produced, and she won an Emmy nomination for her performance in *Roots.* When *I Know Why the Caged Bird Sings* was made into a TV movie, Maya wrote the script and the music. She also wrote and produced a ten-part TV series on African traditions in American life. She has received many honorary degrees, serves on the board of trustees of the American Film Institute, and is Reynolds Professor of American Studies at Wake Forest University in Winston-Salem, North Carolina.

> Literature is my Utopia. Here I am not disenfranchised. No barrier of the sense shuts me from the sweet, gracious discourse of my book friends. They talk to me without embarrassment or awkwardness.
>
> —*Helen Keller*

Her autobiographies have been criticized for not being completely factual, to which she once replied, "There's a world of difference between truth and facts. Facts can obscure the truth. You can tell so many facts that you fill the stage but haven't gotten one iota of truth." The ban notwithstanding, she is deeply respected throughout the country for her amazing capacity not merely to survive, but to triumph.

The ability to control one's own destiny . . . comes from constant hard work and courage.

Maya Angelou

five

Prolific Pens

Indefatigable Ink

THERE ARE THOSE women who, once they have begun writing, cannot be stopped. These writers have drawn upon oceans of ink and forests of paper to create entire libraries of their own. They are an especially amazing breed because, as any of them can tell you, writing is probably one of the loneliest professions—necessitating a good relationship with yourself and full access to the recesses of your imagination. Most of these women have chosen a singular genre, a specific field they till again and again, reaping new characters, crimes more heinous than ever, or still steeper heights of passion.

These women have legions of readers and rabid fan-bases ever eager for the next book and the next book and the next book after that. Dame Barbara Cartland penned more than a thousand original works, earning her the title of the "Queen of Romance." As destiny would have it, life imitated art when she was dubbed a dame by the royals themselves and, by marriage twice over, was related to Princess Diana, whose life and tragic death could have come from the pages of an especially riveting Cartland page-turner.

America's Danielle Steel is her colonial cousin, in spirit, surely. She has written so many bestsellers that she, too, has become as close to a princess as the provinces are capable. She lives in a stately mansion with its own ballroom in San Francisco and, rather recently, has found the love of her life—Hollywood's original "Golden Boy," actor George Hamilton, who left Tinseltown for Baghdad by the Bay to be near his literary love.

And then there's the sisterhood of crime—Agatha Christie, Dorothy Sayers, and Sue Grafton, whose skillful sleuths have become as beloved as the writers themselves, inspiring countless television shows, mini-series, and feature films. Who can forget Angela Lansbury as Miss Marple personified, dominating Sunday night television for years?

What drives an author to write one book after another?

Maybe there is a clue in the unforgettable question asked by Sayers' character Harriet Vane, in her novel *Gaudy Night*, "Do you find it easy to get drunk on words?"

Prolific Pens
Indefatigable Ink

Books . . . are like lobster shells, we surround ourselves with 'em, then we grow out of 'em and leave 'em behind, as evidence of our earlier stages of development.

Dorothy L. Sayers

§ CHRISTINA GEORGINA ROSSETTI

poetic pre-Raphaelite

Women who love
books too much

Well-loved poet Christina Rossetti was born to the arts. Her father, a poet in exile from his home in Italy for his politics, moved to England and taught at King's College. Her two brothers were the equally gifted pre-Raphaelite painter Dante Gabriel Rossetti and William Michael, a poet and editor of a widely known periodical of the day. Christina's older sister, Maria, a writer and scholar of the Italian poet Dante, joined an Anglican order and dedicated her life to serving the needy.

Shyly beautiful and alleged to be hot tempered, Christina was used repeatedly as a model for the Virgin in the memorable paintings of her brother. Her sharp wit was appreciated by the friends her brother Dante Gabriel would invite to their home—Edmund Gusset, William Shields, Sir Edward Coley Burne-Jones, Coventry Patmore, William Morris, Richard Garnett, and Walter Watts-Dunton, as well as writers, political thinkers, and all manner of creative, intelligent people who gathered to exchange views, artistic and otherwise.

Christina pursued poetry passionately. Influenced by John Keats, she wrote prodigiously from a young age. By age seventeen her first collection had been published. She wrote more than 1,100 poems, many resonant of a religious fervor, while both she and her mother worked at a day school to help support the family.

One of the most widely read women writers of her day, achieving both acclaim and respect, Christina fell in love her brother's friend, the artist James Collinson, when she was thirty. But she ultimately

138 turned away from the relationship because of a difference in reli-

gious doctrines. Deeply religious, she had ascetic tendencies, abandoning the game of chess because she was "too eager to win." She wouldn't attend plays (sinful), prayed several times a day, and fasted and confessed regularly. She memorized the Bible and could quote it at length. Ten years after spurning Collinson, Christina gained the affections of her father's student, Charles Bagot Cayley. Once again, his faith didn't meet her approval and she refused her last chance for love and marriage.

At the age of forty-one, she fell ill with Graves disease. Christina kept to herself after that, always writing, until she died from cancer in 1894. On her deathbed, her brother Michael was shocked when his sister screamed out, "My heart then rose a rebel against light." She died as her brother portrayed her, a virgin, her passions poured out on the page.

> *Pain is not pleasure*
> *If we know*
> *It heaps up treasure—*
> *Even so!*
> *Turn, transfigured Pain,*
> *Sweetheart, turn again,*
> *For fair thou art as moonrise after rain.*

Christina Rossetti

§ EDITH WHARTON *"historic ravager"*

Women who love
books too much

I wonder what Edith Wharton, Henry James, and Jane Austen would think if they realized that, long after the span of their own lifetimes, their work rules Hollywood as favorite novels-turned-movies? Henry James, mentor to Edith Wharton, would probably not be surprised at their dominion over the current fascination with social mores. James couldn't seem to reach the heights of his hyperbolic praise for Wharton, calling her "the whirling princess, the great and glorious pendulum, the gyrator, the devil-dancer, the golden eagle, the Fire Bird, the Shining One, the angel of desolation or of devastation, the historic ravager."

Born in 1862 in New York to a wealthy family, Edith Newbold Jones was from the privileged background she described in her novels. She summered in Newport, Rhode Island, and lived abroad—in Italy, Germany, and France—riding out the depression that immediately followed the Civil War and affected her family's fortunes.

BELOVED BOOKS ON WRITING BY WWLBTM

Escaping into the Open by Elizabeth Berg

Writing the Natural Way by Gabriele Lusser Rico

The Writing Life by Annie Dillard (who also deserves mention for her great book *Living by Fiction*)

Writing Down the Bones by Natalie Goldberg

Becoming a Writer by Dorothea Brande

Bird by Bird by Anne Lamott

If You Want to Write by Brenda Ueland

One Continuous Mistake by Gail Sher

She was homeschooled by a governess and prepared for her debut into society at the age of seventeen. Unlike many of her fellow debs, however, Edith Newbold Jones was already writing. The teenager took her craft very seriously, at sweet sixteen producing a volume of poetry that her parents had printed despite their misgivings about her pursuit of writing as a career. She also read insatiably, devouring the books in her father's library; otherwise, she claimed, her "mind would have starved at the age when the mental muscles are most in need of feeding. . . . I was enthralled by words. . . . Wherever I went they sang to me like the birds in an enchanted forest."

In 1885, she married Edward "Teddy" Robbins Wharton, the son of an elite Boston family. Teddy was thirteen years her senior, and they quickly created a life reflecting their genteel parentage. Sadly, Edith's husband was not her intellectual match and had few interests in that direction; he was more interested in having children, which was rapidly becoming a major issue in their marriage. They remained childless and kept up a façade of compatibility to the world.

EDITH WHARTON *Henry James called her "the angel of desolation or of devastation."*

Meanwhile, Edith struggled to write on a level in accordance with her own ambitions, finally getting her inspiration and footing after a voyage through the Greek Isles. She then wrote and published a series of very well-received articles for

Scribner's, Harper's, and *Century,* even collaborating with a Boston architect, Ogden Codman, Jr., on a book entitled *The Decoration of Houses* in 1897. Despite these efforts, she fell into a severe depression she called her "paralyzing melancholy" and had to get a "rest cure" for nervous illnesses.

In 1899, two collections of her short stories were published, coinciding with the end of her nervous condition and depression. After this, she consigned herself over to writing completely and published a book a year for the remainder of her life. In 1905, with *The House of Mirth,* she achieved the height of her power and range as a writer. Subsequent novels, such as *The Reef, The Custom of the Country,* and *The Age of Innocence* caused comparisons to her friend and counselor, as a "female Henry James." She was clearly on her own track, also making a study of symbolists such as Joseph Conrad and the modern musical compositions of Igor Stravinsky.

Edith Wharton began an affair with a member of her literary circle, James' protégé Morton Fullerton. While the Wharton marriage crumbled around them, they sold their stately Lenox home, "The Mount," and moved to France. Teddy Wharton suffered a nervous breakdown and checked into a Swiss sanatorium, divorcing Edith in 1913. She remained in Europe, making a home for herself in France.

Edith Wharton found the life of a divorcée to be revelatory. She could travel, entertain, write, and have friendships with men without any interference. She also got involved in public and political affairs and, among her significant charity works, founded shelters for refugees during World War I.

In 1930, Edith Wharton was elected to the National Institute of Arts and Letters and, four years later, to the American Academy of Arts and Letters. She lived to the age of seventy-five, when she had a fatal stroke. During her life of letters, she contributed enormously to the novel form. Her subtlety and sophistication continue to bring her books to many readers, far beyond the bounds of the new elite in Hollywood.

> *The books ARE in bad shape, and as some are interesting it's a pity. I told Miss Hatchard they were suffering from dampness and lack of air. . . . I'm so fond of old books that I'd rather see them made into bonfire than left to moulder away like these.*

Edith Wharton, from *Summer*

§ MARGARET MEAD *no stopping her*

Margaret Mead still stirs controversy in some circles for her pioneering work in social anthropology. Like Rachel Carson, she wrote a scientific study that crossed over into the general population and became a bestseller. For this, she received derision from the academic community. But that didn't bother the free spirit, who was one of the first women to earn a Ph.D. in anthropology.

Margaret was fortunate to be born in 1901 into a family of academics who disregarded convention and put learning and involvement in the world ahead of society's rules. The firstborn of five children, Margaret was the child of Edward Mead, a professor who taught finance and economics at the University of Pennsylvania, and Emily Fogg Mead, a teacher, sociologist, and ardent feminist and suffragist. Margaret was homeschooled by her very able grandmother, a former teacher and school principal.

Margaret didn't fall too far from the tree when she started The Minority, an anti-fraternity at DePauw University, where she was attending. Bored, she transferred to Barnard College, where the academic standards were more in accordance with her needs. Originally an English major, in her senior year Margaret attended a class given by anthropologist Franz Boas, a virulent opponent of the school of racial determinism. She also met Ruth Benedict, then Boas' assistant, who encouraged Margaret to join her at Columbia under Boas' instruction. Margaret agreed and went on to graduate school after marriage to a seminary student, Luther Cressman. Soon after, true to her heritage as a free-thinking Mead, Margaret went against her mentor Boas' urgings that she do fieldwork with America's Native peoples, a pet project of his; instead she followed the beat of her own different and, as it turns out, tribal drums, setting off for Polynesia to explore island cultures. She reasoned that the islanders were better subjects because they had been less exposed and, therefore, less assimilated than Native Americans.

She was absolutely right. She wrote up her field studies after living with and working alongside the Samoans for three years. The date was 1926. Divorcing Luther, she married Reo Fortune, and in 1928 published *Coming of Age in Samoa,* a groundbreaking work that shocked some circles for its frank and completely objective report of, among other things, the sexual rituals and practices among the Samoans. Nearly overnight, Margaret was a superstar, fairly rare for anthropologists and even rarer for twenty-seven-year-old female anthropologists!

After a stint in the American Museum of Natural History, Margaret headed to New Guinea. Her resulting book, *Growing Up in New Guinea,* was another huge hit in both academic and popular circles. While in New Guinea, Margaret met and fell in love with fellow anthropologist Gregory Bateson; after her second divorce she and Gregory married, and she gave birth to her daughter, Mary Catherine Bateson. They worked together in New Guinea, but ultimately Gregory claimed she was stifling his creativity, and they divorced in 1943.

Margaret Mead spent the rest of her life working full-tilt in anthropology. She was astonishingly prolific, publishing forty-four books and more than 1,000 articles and monographs, and working

as a curator at the American Museum of Natural History between trips to the field. She also sought to support the work of young anthropologists. At the core of all of her work was an analysis of childhood development (she was the first anthropologist ever to study childrearing practices) and gender roles, overturning many time-worn assumptions about personality and place in society for both sexes. Again and again, her studies demonstrated that there is nothing natural or universal about particular "masculine" or "feminine" roles; rather they are culturally determined.

In her later years, she wrote a wonderful autobiography, *Blackberry Winter*, that contains her reflections on her childhood as well as the field-

MARGARET MEAD *To some of her fellow academics,* Coming of Age in Samoa *was a sexy shocker!*

work methods she developed. Through her prodigious output, average people came to read about and reflect on the lives of those they had previously considered "strange."

I have spent most of my life studying the lives of other peoples, faraway peoples, so that Americans might better understand themselves.

Margaret Mead

§ IRIS MURDOCH *fiction's philosopher*

Jean Iris Murdoch was born in Dublin in 1919. By the time of her death in 1998, she was regarded as one of the finest writers in the English language. Unlike many of her peers, she was able to cross genres and wrote philosophy and literary criticism in addition to the novels for which she became adored.

She was part of a writer's clique with fellow upstarts William Golding, author of *Lord of the Flies,* and Kingsley Amis, who authored *Lucky Jim.* Iris' first effort was *Under the Net.* She and her cohorts' books were all published in 1954, a banner year for new British fiction. The trio took their writing very seriously, as Iris explains in several essays in which she defines their work as an important new "liberal" school of fiction, following in the heritage of the "best fiction makers," such as Jane Austen, George Eliot, and Leo Tolstoy's "absurd irreducible uniqueness of people and of their relations with each other." Murdoch argued, very effectively, that the darlings of the day, Imagists T. S. Eliot and Ezra Pound, confined characters and readers in a dry, feelingless vacuum. Murdoch, on the other hand, believed life as lived by real people to be much less tidy and much more filled with emotions, and that is vitally important that this freedom be allowed experientially though fiction, written for a "community of free beings."

Although Jean-Paul Sartre and Murdoch might seem strange bedfellows at first, she drew much philosophic and creative inspiration from his existentialism and his avowed dedication to the cause of freedom. In London, she had studied economics and, at Somerville College in Oxford, did her graduate work in classical humanities, which included studying the "great" Greek and Latin philosophers. She met Sartre in Belgium during World War II, when she was a young woman working in England's civil service. In 1947, she won a scholarship to attend Cambridge and met another major figure in twentieth-century philosophy, Ludwig Wittgenstein, whose beliefs were to become undercurrents in *Under the Net*, particularly his now-famous dictum from Tractatus, "Whereof we can not speak, thereof we must remain silent."

Another core Murdoch tenet in both her philosophical and fiction writing is respect for other people's differences, especially in love relationships. She claimed her novels' *raison d'être* is drawn from Sartre's "breath-taking argument" for the novel. In 1953, she wrote a tract, *Sartre: Romantic Rationalist,* one of several nonfiction works that also included *The Sovereignty of Good* and *The Fire and the Sun: Why Plato Banished the Artists,* wherein she delineates her keen interest in "goodness" outside religious restrictions, a doctrine she explained late in life as "mysticism" without the presence of God.

Murdoch found such beliefs to be fertile ground for her more than two dozen novels and countless essays; indeed her aim was to place art over philosophy, believing that it is art that expresses ultimate truth. She lived a peaceful life with her husband, critic John Bayley, in a small country village in England. Bayley, who shared her interests and philosophies, has written a lovely memoir of their last years together, when she began her decline due to Alzheimer's disease, telling how he chose to care for her himself instead of installing her in a nursing home.

Now, after her death, Iris Murdoch, the friend, the wife, the philosopher, and the novelist, continues to be cherished for her uniqueness and for the gifts she so freely shared.

Art is about the pilgrimage from appearance to reality.

Iris Murdoch

---

§ DOROTHY L. SAYERS *mystery maven*

Born in 1893, Dorothy Sayers is one of England's most revered writers, particularly for her twelve detective novels. But she also wrote twenty works of poetry, critical essays, and plays in addition to her popular fiction, and penned forty-four short stories.

Oxford-educated, where she earned honors in medieval studies and was one of the first women ever to earn a degree, she taught for several years and then gained work as a reader for publisher Basil Blackwell. Her first publication was a volume of her poetry published during this period. Sayers changed jobs in the 1920s and went to work for an advertising agency, and also made another important shift in hobbies by joining the Detection Club. This enterprise, which included fellow member G. K. Chesterton, was dedicated to raising the reputation and quality of detective fiction.

SUE GRAFTON *W Is for writer*

What is mystery writer Sue Grafton going to do when she finishes with the alphabet? Born in Louisville, Kentucky, on April 24, 1940, she lived there through college, where she studied literature at the local university. Before she found her fortune in writing detective fiction, she worked as a cashier, an admissions clerk, and a medical secretary. Struggling to support herself and three children, Grafton wrote seven novels, mostly unpublished, before she came up with her winning formula in 1982 with *A is for Alibi.* Her fifteen alphabetical novels (she's finished O at this writing) are now published in twenty-eight countries and twenty-six languages, creating readerships in such places as Bulgaria, Estonia, and India. She has reframed the alphabet for devotees of her spunky female detective character, Kinsey Millhone, with *B is for Burglar, C is for Corpse, D is for Deadbeat, E is for Evidence,* and so on. Fans worry about "life after Z."

So there I was barreling down the highway in search of employment and not at all fussy about what kind I'd take.

—Sue Grafton

Dorothy Sayers was most effective at improving the genre by her own efforts, and for the next twenty years became the top writer in detective fiction. Her first novel was *Whose Body?,* released in 1923; eight years later, she was making a good living solely from her witty, sophisticated novels.

Her recurring character is Lord Peter Wimsey, an aristocrat who did sleuthing as a pastime. Clearly a favorite of both Sayers and her readers, Lord Wimsey is present in all but one of her detective novels. Another recurring character is Harriet Vane, a woman sleuth based on the author herself, who provided equal opportunity for both genders in the genre that had become her domain. After writing *Busman's Honeymoon* in 1937, she turned to composing religious scripts for radio and essays on a multitude of topics such as theology and—what else?—murder mysteries.

Dorothy Sayers' *Five Red Herrings* is regarded as one of the classics of its kinds, and her oeuvre continues to sell briskly more than forty years after her death in 1957.

> *Allow me to inform you that I never at any time either sought or desired an Oxford fellowship. . . . Neither was I "forced" into either the publishing or the advertising profession. . . . Nor do I quite understand why earning one's living should be represented as a hardship. 'Intellectual frustration' be blowed! . . . It was all very good fun while it lasted.*
>
> Dorothy L. Sayers, in a 1955 letter to the
> *Church Times,* which had erroneously
> described her as a wannabe Oxford don

§ BARBARA CARTLAND
the world's best-known romance writer

Barbara Cartland's status as a preeminent "prolific pen" is doubtless: she wrote 623 books and sold more than 650 million copies of her novels worldwide in many languages. Even *The Guinness Book of World Records* named her as the world's top-selling author! Upon her passing on May 20, 2000, she remained the twentieth century's best-known writer of romance.

Born on July 9, 1901, this British writer went on to dominate popular fiction throughout the century. She began her writing career with a gossip column in the *Daily Express* newspaper, an ironic choice for a woman who would become the relative of one of the most gossiped-about women in the history of the world, Princess Diana. By 1925, Cartland had moved to full fiction with her debut novel, *Jigsaw,* and had been presented at court. From this beginning, she released new novels at a furious pace, with such titles

as *The Ruthless Rake, The Penniless Peer,* and *The Cruel Count,* as well as several volumes of autobiography and other nonfiction works, such as *The Etiquette Book; Love, Life, and Sex; Look Lovely, Be Lovely;* and *Barbara Cartland's Book of Beauty and Health,* for which she received strong criticism due to a very old-fashioned, rather antifeminist view of women as the "inferior" gender.

This dissatisfaction passed quickly, though, and Barbara retained her crown as the world-renowned queen of romance novels. In 1950 she moved to Camfield Place, the house built by Beatrix Potter's grandfather, where Potter wrote "The Tale of Peter Rabbit." Many movies have been based on

BARBARA CARTLAND *Princess Diana's aunt by marriage, this hardworking author of 623 books never rested on her laurels.*

her beloved books, including *A Hazard of Hearts, A Duel of Hearts, The Flame Is Love, The Ghost of Monte Carlo,* and *The Lady and the Highwayman,* and her position at the "top of the heap" is in no danger. No other writer has written so much for so many as Dame Barbara Cartland.

TAKING ROMANCE SERIOUSLY

Romance readers love their books—romance books generate approximately $1 billion in sales yearly. And romance writers are passionate about their genre.

Founded in Houston, Texas, in 1980 by thirty-seven authors frustrated with writing conferences that seemed to ignore romance writers, the Romance Writers of America has grown into the largest national genre writers' association in the world. According to their Web site, the organization "provides networking and support to individuals seriously pursuing a career in romance fiction," and its 8,000-member organization is now "considered 'The Voice of Romance.'" In 1999, RWA had more than 120 chapters throughout the world. Each summer it hosts a national conference with more than 100 workshops and gives annual awards. To find out more, contact their Web site (**www.rwanational.com**), e-mail them at info@rwanational.com, or call (281) 440-6885.

§ MARGARET ATWOOD *oracle of Ottawa*

On at least one occasion, prodigious writer Margaret Atwood has mentioned the comic book fantasies she read as a child in Ottawa as her primary influences, but she seems much more closely linked to the Victorians she studied in her postgraduate work at Harvard.

Prolific Pens
Indefatigable Ink

Born in Ottawa in 1939, she traveled with her entomologist father into remote areas of northern Canada and the bush of Quebec. Educated at the University of Toronto, Radcliffe, and Harvard, she was drawn to writing at a young age and began to publish her poetry by the age of nineteen.

Atwood's writing often delves into the mythic, retelling Homer's *Ulysses,* for example, from the vantage point of the women who were seduced and left behind. Her novels, including *The Edible Woman; Surfacing; Lady Oracle; Life Before Man; The Handmaid's Tale;* and *Alias Grace,* give voice to such silenced voices. The natural world is another major theme for Atwood, as are her unique twists on the psychological. Her published work includes nine novels, four children's books, twenty-three volumes of poetry, and four works of scholarship. She also is the editor of five anthologies. A film based on *The Handmaid's Tale* was released in 1990.

MARGARET ATWOOD *Canada's mythic naturalist and novelist.*

In addition to being prolific, she is also among the most awarded writers, receiving more than 100 prizes for her excellent poetry and fiction. Moreover, she is claimed by her country of origin, Canada, as helping establish an identity for Canadian literature. Her work in the 1970s for Aanansi Press very directly aided this cause. *Survival,* which she wrote in 1972, was an attempt at a "a map" for charting Canada's writers, followed by *The Oxford Book of Canadian Verse* in 1982. Her sense of place is often a theme in her fiction and poems. Strong women rising against all odds appear again and again in her work, underlining her heroine's final words in *Surfacing:* "This above all, to refuse to be a victim."

> *I'm not a very good gardener, for the same reason I wouldn't make a very good poisoner: both activities benefit from advance planning.*
>
> Margaret Atwood, from *Various Gardens*

ATWOOD ONLINE

Those who wish to pursue their interest in Atwood's work have a variety of Web sources to choose from. She herself has a site—the Margaret Atwood Information Page (222.web.net/owtoad)—in which you can read interviews, see her answers to frequently asked questions, and even get a list of her favorite quotes. And be sure to check out The Unofficial Shrine of Margaret Atwood at **sac.uky.edu/ ~jrdona0/MA/welcome.html**, maintained by a big fan.

§ DANIELLE STEEL *solid gold Steel*

America's sweetheart, Danielle Steel is one of the hardest working women in the book business. She has a unique approach, differing from other prolific writers who claim to focus on one project at a time. She works on up to five books at a time, juggling storylines, writing one and editing others. Add her movie scripts and adaptations from her fiction and you have a virtuoso at work, and very successfully. Make no mistake, however, her books are not "cranked out"; her research process alone usually takes at least three years. Once she has fully studied her subjects in preparing to dive into a book, she can spend up to eighteen to twenty hours nonstop at her 1946 Olympia typewriter.

Prolific Pens
Indefatigable Ink

Steel hails from New York and was sent to France for her education. Upon graduation, she worked in the public relations and advertising industries. She left these to craft a career as a writer and, clearly, found the work she was best suited for. She also married and raised nine children. Never considered particularly feminist, Steel creates female protagonists in her romance novels that are powerful women, often driven career women, who juggle work, life, and love. *Palomino*, published in 1981, is centered around a woman rancher who founds a center for handicapped children; *Kaleidoscope* is the story of an orphan girl who survives a series of foster homes, and recovers from rape to track down her sisters and reunite her family.

The statistics about Danielle Steel's career are staggering: 390 million copies of books in print, nearly fifty *New York Times* bestselling novels, and a series of "Max and Martha" illustrated books for children to help them deal with difficult issues such as death, new babies, divorce, moving, new schools, and other real-life problems. She has written a volume of love poems, and her 1998 book about the death of her son Nicholas Traina, *His Bright Light*, shot to the top of the *New York Times* nonfiction bestselling list upon its release. At this point, twenty-eight of her books have been adapted for films, and one, *Jewels*, garnered two Golden Globe nominations. She is listed in *The Guinness Book of World Records* for the amazing run of one of her titles on the *Times* bestseller list for 381 weeks straight. Since that, another has beaten her own record with 390 consecutive weeks.

Danielle Steel doesn't rest on her many laurels or her beauty, wealth, fame, and unstoppable talent. She also works diligently on behalf of various charities—she serves as the National Chairperson for the American Library Association, on the National Committee for the Prevention of Child Abuse, and as spokesperson for the American Humane Association.

Not content with a villa, a loving family, and a view of the Golden Gate Bridge, Danielle Steel realizes her readers are her most important resource and has made herself accessible to them via e-mail through her publisher, Random House. While she is often compared to the fictional heroines of her own invention, her life is undoubtedly much quieter. But, if she does have anything in common with them, it is her strength of will and her inimitable style. There is only *one* Danielle Steel.

> *I believe in dreams, not just the kind we have at night. I think that if we hang onto them, they come true.*
>
> Danielle Steel

§ JOYCE CAROL OATES *her heart laid bare*

Seemingly, Joyce Carol Oates can turn her hand to any subject and inject it with her trademark multilayered depth. She is well on her way to becoming one of the world's most abundant artists, having authored, as of this writing, forty-one novels and novellas, twenty-five collections of short stories, eight volumes of poetry, nine collections of essays (including one on boxing), and has edited thirteen

prestigious anthologies, most notably the *Norton Anthology of Contemporary Fiction.*

While she crosses barriers of time frequently in her novels, from postmodern urban settings to the Victorian era and back again, and works in genres from Gothic to realism, she does have one overriding theme: violence. From prostitutes to primordial goddess figures (her novel, *Blonde,* based on the life of Marilyn Monroe, was published to raves in March 2000), her writing fascinates as much as it shocks. She has received a fair amount of criticism for the disturbance in her fiction, but she explains it thusly: "The more violent the murders in *Macbeth,* the more relief one can feel at *not* having to perform them. Great art is cathartic; it is always moral."

JOYCE CAROL OATES *Artist of the macabre.*

She was born in Lockport, New York, to an Irish Catholic family of modest means. Joyce's intelligence saw her to the head of most classes, and she graduated Phi Beta Kappa from Syracuse University before doing her master's work in English literature at the University of Wisconsin. Her writing talent was noted early—she won the *Mademoiselle* fiction contest while still in college.

A reportedly excellent teacher, she has taught at several schools, most recently at Princeton, with her husband, academic Raymond Smith, while maintaining her grueling writing schedule. Her body of work averages a novel every two years, beginning in 1963; she has been known, however, to publish a book a year.

When asked how she manages to produce such critically acclaimed work so quickly, she told the *New York Times,* "I have always lived a very conventional life of moderation, absolutely regular hours, nothing exotic, no need, even, to organize my time." When labeled a workaholic by a reporter, she retorted, "I am not conscious of working especially hard, or of 'working' at all. Writing and teaching have always been, for me, so richly rewarding that I don't think of them as work in the usual sense of the word."

> *To read widely and to be open and curious about other people, to look and listen hard, not to be discouraged by rejections—we've all had them many times—and revise your work.*
>
> Joyce Carol Oates' advice to other writers

SIX

Salonists and Culture Makers

Hermeneutic Circles and Human History

A LOOK AT CULTURAL turning points throughout history reveals an interesting pattern: often a small circle of friends was the crucial point of origin for a revolutionary change in art, politics, or philosophy. In his definitive study of early modernism, *American Salons,* Robert W. Crunden states that "major changes in human attitude have small beginnings," and indeed, from the pre-Raphaelites to the Romantics, from the Surrealists to the suffragists, and from the Harlem Renaissance to the Beats, intimate gatherings of friends were at the heart of nearly every significant new movement.

The very nature of salons—organic, informal, and relational—made women central to these groupings. Before women could vote or own property, they were part and parcel of this kind of culture making. In Paris, the Surrealists welcomed women as equals, while modernist Gertrude Stein opened her ample home and heart to struggling male artists like Matisse and Picasso, as well as upstart writers like Ernest Hemingway and Paul Bowles. Party girl-intellectual Joan Burroughs hosted a gaggle of charming college dropouts—Allen Ginsberg, William Burroughs, and Jack Kerouac—in her Manhattan apartment, doling out champagne and Spengler in equal servings, as her predecessor Mabel Dodge had in Greenwich Village forty years before.

One writer, Jean Shinoda Bolen, author of *Goddesses in Everywoman,* suggests this phenomena is no accident. In *The Millionth Circle: How to Change Ourselves and the World,* she proposes that salons, circles, and book discussion groups are actually the key to the evolution of humanity, for "when a critical number of people change how they think and behave, the culture will also, and a new era begins." Think about that when you and your girlfriends sip cappuccinos while chatting about your favorite new novel— you are changing the world!

§ MADAME ROLAND *priestess of the revolution*

That women intellectuals in turn-of-the-century France suffered during the French Revolution is without a doubt. Madame de Staël was exiled for her politics; while Madame Jeanne-Marie Roland lost her head entirely.

Roland's father was a laborer, an engraver. Her humble origins, however, did not stop her from becoming one of the pivotal players in the French Revolution, going on to hold great power in the government of her day. While Betsy Ross was sewing stripes onto the flag of the fledgling United States, this French workman's daughter commanded the helm of her country.

Jeanne-Marie Phlipon was politically precocious. Listening raptly while her father waged a verbal war against the French aristocracy, his opinions were engraved upon her sensibility and she began educating herself for a life of civic action. At the age of nine, she read Plutarch; his *Lives* made her wish she had lived in classical Rome, with its senatorial lectures and truth-seeking philosophers. Meanwhile, Jean-Jacques Rousseau was stirring the hearts and minds of his readers with his egalitarian theories, which the young girl devoured as well.

Her idealistic father's fortunes took an unfortunate turn during Jeanne-Marie's adolescence, when he lost all his earnings in stock and became a compulsive gambler. Left with nothing but his daughter's dowry, he lived off that, drank himself into dissolution, and refused her hand to Roland de la Platière, whom she met through a convent-school friend. Roland was not the only man in pursuit of the handsome, strong-willed Jeanne-Marie, with her dark, burning eyes and raven hair. However, this suitor was not easily dissuaded and continued his quest for marriage to the bookish girl. Platière came from considerable wealth, but retained a position as an inspector at a factory. Although he was nearly twice her age, they had quite a bit in common, especially a love of classic literature. In later life, Madame Roland claimed, "He was a man fond of ancient history, and more like the ancients than the modern; about seven and forty years old, stooping and awkward and with manners respectable rather than pleasing."

Their shared life of the mind won out over her other admirers, and they married when she was twenty-five. They began an earnest relationship of respect and erudition. Her feelings about her marriage are indicated in this diary entry from her wedding day: "I could make a model of a man I could love, but it would be shattered the moment he became my master." While theirs was a marriage of minds, Jeanne-Marie eventually found romance elsewhere with Henri Buzot, her companion until her death.

Immediately after her marriage, stirrings of revolution were evident. Madame Roland associated herself with the Girondists, named for the district from which their leaders came, who favored a republic, supported the abolition of the constitutional monarchy, and opposed the violence of the Terror. The Girondists soon became the majority party, dominating the government of France during their height. Led by Jacques Pierre Brissot, they believed in the ownership of private property. The newlyweds both involved themselves deeply in the revolution and opened their home to meetings that rapidly evolved into a salon run by Madame Roland, which she made open to all different elements of revolutionary thinking.

Roland recorded in her journals the fascinating discussions that

took place at these events; she also began writing essays and voluminous letters to her fellows. Along with Georges Danton, a member of the Girondist's opposition, the Jacobins, Robespierre frequented the salon and was greatly influenced by Roland, most famously when he made a speech to the National Assembly espousing theories she taught him, in language in which he had been coached by her. Both husband and wife attended the National Assembly of France, and Madame wrote newspaper articles as well as her husband's speeches and official state documents.

She was a woman who knew the powerful effect her writing could have. When the Austrian army, accompanied by escaped

MADAME ROLAND DE LA PLATIÈR *Jailed and guillotined during the French Revolution's "Reign of Terror."*

French aristocrats, gathered at the border to invade the weakened, split country, Madame Roland wrote King Louis XVI urging him to declare war in kind; he struck her husband from office. But the consequences of his refusal to do as she suggested ultimately cost the king his crown and his head. The tumult increased; Roland's wealth caused him to be suspected and arrested during the purge of the ruling class. A split between two factions, the Girondists and the Jacobins, occurred when the Jacobins laid blame on the Girondists for the defeats against the war on Austria. The Jacobins' retribution was swift and brutal; they guillotined Brissot and thirty others, arresting the remaining factionalists.

The Girondists had espoused moderation, but conceded in the vote to execute King Louis XVI and Marie Antoinette, while fighting against the siege tactics of Marat and Robespierre. Her former salonist and student Robespierre began to plot against the articulate and charismatic Madame Roland and betrayed her, resulting in her imprisonment in a dungeon cell into which the River Seine seeped. Sadly, Robespierre's and Madame Roland's relationship, based originally on free exchange, ended tragically out of balance—she saved him from the guillotine while he gave her up to execution.

The same friend who had introduced Madame Roland to her husband offered to change clothes with her and take her place in prison. Roland's refusal was typically elegant: "Better to suffer a thousand deaths myself than to reproach myself with yours." In prison, she suffered horribly. Sick and wasting, she was thrown in with prostitutes, murders, and thieves; she used her gift of language to appeal to the doomed women prisoners to stop their riots and

cease their violence against each other.

Born in Scotland in 1801, Jane Welsh was the daughter of a physician who practiced in London. Her enlightened and intelligent father saw to it that Jane was given the best available education, grounding her in the classics beginning at the age of five. Her instructor Edward Irving was deeply impressed with Jane's brilliance and, in 1821, introduced her to Thomas Carlyle, a reputed historian and writer. When she turned twenty-five, she married Carlyle; together they were at the center of a circle of English artists, writers, and thinkers. Known for her intelligence and charm, she made fast friends with Geraldine Jewsbury and hosted such luminaries as Charles Dickens, John Stuart Mill, and Lord Tennyson.

Jane was an inveterate letter writer, filling her missives with wit, keen observations, and real feeling. She is viewed as elevating writing letters to an art form, covering every conceivable topic from travel and books to friends, servants, and acute descriptions of personality. Her letters are published in several volumes, revealing the marital dysfunction that pressed enormous strain on Jane. Her husband had great ambition as a writer but they lived in poverty, with Jane suffering Thomas' neglect and irritability. Fearing a mental breakdown, she suddenly collapsed and died in 1866 while riding in a carriage.

In less than a month's time she wrote her memoirs in prison. The officials presiding over her trial were so afraid of Madame Roland's facility with words, they refused her to "use her wit" and ordered her only to answer the questions put to her with yes or no. She was, of course, convicted and hastened to the guillotine in just twelve hours. One other prisoner was put to the blade that day, a terrified printer for whom she argued for a peculiar kind of mercy; she asked he be executed first to spare him the awful sight of seeing   167 her head roll. A clay model of the Statue of Liberty was placed near the scaffold to which Madame Roland addressed her famous last words, "O Liberty! What crimes have been committed in thy name!" She died on November 8, 1793, at the age of thirty-nine.

§ MERET OPPENHEIM *Surrealist savant*

Paris, the City of Lights, seemed to be the most fertile ground for artists and writers in the early twentieth century. Several salons and schools of thought formed there, leaving an indelible mark upon culture at large. Artist and poet Meret Oppenheim found equal footing for her creativity among the Surrealists.

Meret was born in Germany in 1913, and her family moved from Berlin to Weisenthal, Switzerland, when she was five years old; she was schooled in Germany and Switzerland until she was seventeen. At nineteen, she moved to Paris to attend art school, whereupon she immediately fell in with kindred creatives—dancers, philosophers, painters, and poets—who formed a salon of the first wave of Surrealists, a literary and artistic movement that sought to reveal a reality above or beneath ordinary reality. She was befriended by Hans and Sophie Tauber-Arp, Marcel Duchamp, and Alberto Giacometti, who encouraged her to experiment with different media. In 1933, she was asked to exhibit with the Surrealists at Salon des Surindependents. After a successful debut show, Oppenheim's art was featured in all of this group's important exhibitions, beginning with Cubism-Surrealism in 1935. She tried her hand at jewelry making for the great fashion houses of Paris; she made a copper bracelet lined with sealskin and showed it to Pablo Picasso, who remarked, "Many things could be covered in fur." His remark inspired Meret Oppenheim to do just that.

The following year, Oppenheim's *Dejeuner en fourrure (The Fur Tea Cup)* stunned the art world, set off a scandal for its sexy suggestiveness and established the twenty-three-year-old as one of the key figures in Surrealism. When the Museum of Modern Art in New York purchased her teacup sculpture, her standing was cemented. Oppenheim felt the Surrealists were more evolved sociologically, and though this school was mainly male, they welcomed her as an artist completely. A muse for Man Ray, his luminous nude photographs of her are now part of the legacy of Surrealism. When she and Max Ernst met and fell in love, she broke the affair off despite the intensity of their feelings for each other. A long time after, she claimed it was an instinct to protect her growth as a fledgling artist from being squelched by him, a fully mature artist of international reputation.

Though she was a fine poet as well, everything else Meret Oppenheim did was overshadowed by *The Fur Tea Cup,* which shot her into stratospheric fame at the very beginning of her career. Finding herself the "darling of the art world" overnight was awkward, and she suffered deep bouts of depression. The next two decades were very difficult for her in terms of her work; after an early and meteoric rise to success, she found herself a "has-been" nearly from the start.

She left Paris for Basel during the aftermath of her sudden fame, and undertook years of Jungian analysis to help her understand her depression. In 1949, she married a businessman, Wolfgang La Roche, who supported her need for independence, and she spent weekends at her studio in Berne writing, making art, and reading a great deal,

SYLVIA BEACH *bookseller extraordinaire*

American Sylvia Beach was captivated by Paris the first time she saw it in the early 1900s. But it wasn't until after World War I, in 1919, that she established her soon-to-be-famous bookshop, Shakespeare and Company, which specialized in American and English books. Quickly it became a haven for American expatriates, including Ernest Hemingway and Gertrude Stein, "the" spot for American tourists to visit, and a place where European scholars became more familiar with American and English literature. In 1922, Beach became a publisher as well, printing James Joyce's *Ulysses* after it had been rejected by a myriad of publishers for being obscene. In 1941, she shut down the store in order to avoid takeover by the Nazis during World War II, and it was never opened again. If you ever travel through Newport, Oregon, stop in at the Sylvia Beach Hotel, named for this great literary patron. It offers three categories of rooms—Bestsellers, Novels, and Classics—each named for a famous writer (Agatha Christie, Herman Melville, and Edgar Allen Poe, to mention just three) and containing a complete set of books by that author. The hotel can be reached at (541) 265-5428.

particularly the works of Carl Jung, a friend of the family. She maintained some links with friends from her early salon years and designed costumes for a Picasso ballet in 1956. Proving she could still shock, Meret Oppenheim put together the symbolist installation *Banquet* in 1959, featuring a nude woman as the centerpiece for the table. She lived to see herself "rediscovered" in 1967, enjoying a retrospective in Stockholm, where she regained her reputation and international standing.

Meret Oppenheim was a deeply sensitive woman who mined her unconscious for inspiration and insight. Both her writing and her art reflected her interest in archetypal imagery. She recorded her dreams for most of her life and strove to prove that art of any kind, whether poetry, painting, or sculpture, should have no gender.

> *During my long crisis, my genius, the animus, the*
> *male part of the female soul, that assists the female*
> *artist, had abandoned me. . . . But at the beginning*
> *of the fifties, I sensed that things were getting better.*

Meret Oppenheim

---

§ GERTRUDE AND ALICE *"the mama of Dada"*

Gertrude Stein was a writer who seems to have been imminently comfortable in her own skin and well aware of her fame. Her wholly original writing style shocked and fascinated readers, prompting some wags to dub her "the Mama of Dada" and "the Mother Goose of Montparnasse," but she had her own distinct view: "Einstein was the creative philosophic mind of the century and I have been the creative literary mind of the century." Her influence is still felt in our culture, and of the modernists, she still seems the most starkly modern.

Fitting people with books is about as difficult as fitting them with shoes.

Sylvia Beach

An American whose German-Jewish family moved to Baltimore from Bavaria, Gertrude Stein's father founded a successful clothing business and moved around a good bit with his wife and young children. The brood lived in Austria and Paris before settling in

1879, when Gertrude was four, in Oakland, California, the home about which she made the famously misunderstood comment, "There's no there there." (She meant that her home as she remembered it wasn't there, but the sentence was bandied about as a put-down of the Northern California city for decades.) The brilliant girl spoke German and French, but quickly made English her first language by voraciously reading England's history, poetry, fiction, and, an odd choice for a young girl, congressional records. Gertrude's mother passed away in 1888, when Gertrude was fourteen, followed by her father in 1891, bonding her and her brother, Leo, very closely together under the care of their maternal aunt Fannie Bachrach in Baltimore.

Leo Stein was at Harvard; when it came time to go to college, Gertrude studied under special dispensation at Radcliffe College to be near Leo. Among her teachers there were William James, a pioneer in psychology, and philosopher George Santayana. James took Gertrude under his wing and supported her in her desire to study medicine at Johns Hopkins University in Baltimore. She did obstetrical work in addition to her medical training, and she received support from two wealthy friends, Etta and Claribal Cone.

By 1899, she sank into a severe melancholy and abandoned her study of medicine. Her depression was believed by biographers to be as result of the break-up of a love triangle with May Bookstaver and Mabel Haynes, fictionalized in *Q.E.D., or Things as They Are* (published in 1950, after Stein's death). In 1902 she joined Leo in Italy, where he was pursuing a career in art under the tutelage of Bernard Berenson, and ultimately followed him to Paris. Their flat in the house at 27 rue de Fleurus soon became a famous address in avant-
garde circles, with the duo holding regular salons to which all the art

and literature "glitterati" flocked, including Picasso, Juan Gris, and F. Scott Fitzgerald.

Here Gertrude was exposed to the modern art she so loved and began buying at a rapid pace. A story she loved to tell was the memory of seeing Matisse's *Le Femme au Chapeau* at a Petit Palais show where enraged patrons heckled the painter and tried to destroy the painting by scraping the paint off the surface. Gertrude acquired a stunning collection of Impressionist and Post-Impressionist art,

including works by Renoir, Matisse, Picasso, Rousseau, Braque, and Cézanne. She claimed her attraction to this art was its method of clarification by deformation, an approach some would say she applied to her writing, which was an attempt at a verbal counterpart to Cubism. She eschewed normal punctuation and grammar, and used words associatively and for their sound rather than for meaning. Her goal was to present impressions and states of mind, rather than a story.

However, she also undertook *The Making of Americans,* an attempt to record a history of every type of human. Her early work of 1909, *Three Lives,* was written while she sat for Picasso's portrait of her. As usual, modesty was not her

GERTRUDE STEIN *Along with Alice B. Toklas, she hosted Pablo Picasso, Ernest Hemingway, F. Scott Fitzgerald, Paul Bowles, the ladies of the Left Bank, the Impressionists, and the Surrealists in a nonstop salon.*

strong suit; she proclaimed *Three Lives* to be "the first definite step away from the nineteenth century and into the twentieth century in literature." She asked a new acquaintance, Alice B. Toklas, to proofread the manuscript when she at long last found a publisher. They soon became fast friends and lovers, Alice moving into the atelier once inhabited by Leo Stein. Gertrude's tie to her brother seemed to matter much less with the arrival of San Francisco native Toklas, Gertrude writing, "It was I who was the genius, there was no reason for it but I was and he was not.'

Women who love books too much

The union of the two women seemed to be the mating of souls. Toklas founded Plain Edition Press to publish Stein's many unpublished manuscripts, and Stein's writing took on new strength, rhythm, and feeling, with her erotic writings based on their relationship. Popular success evaded Stein, however, until she wrote, in Toklas' voice, *The Autobiography of Alice B. Toklas* in 1933. This charming "autobiography" tells of the salon they hosted—the young writers Stein mentored, Sherwood Anderson and Ernest Hemingway, and discloses delicious gossip about the bevy of artists in their circle. This was less amusing to the artists themselves, prompting *The Testimony against Gertrude Stein,* a refutation of her comments, wherein Braque accused her of not understanding Cubism, Matisse railed against her lack of taste, and Tristan Tzara decried her "megalomania" and her egotism as evidenced by such statements of Stein's as, "Think of the Bible and Homer, think of Shakespeare and think of me." Among the most fascinating episodes in the *Autobiography* is the ambulance service the two women ran in World War I, which they seemed to regard as high adventure.

Gertrude Stein's reputation as a major influence on new forms in literature was growing. She began to write novels and plays, including *Four Saints in Three Acts,* and she was invited to do lecture tours at the most prestigious venues: Oxford, Cambridge, and in America, with the operatic staging of her play. The Second World War forced Stein and Toklas to leave Paris and set up a more permanent home in the country near Bilignin, where they entertained many American soldiers. In 1946, she was diagnosed with an abdominal tumor and was hospitalized at the American Hospital at Neuilly-sur-Seine. Her last words are part of her legacy. She regained consciousness for a few moments after stomach surgery and asked, "What is the answer?" No one responded, and Gertrude Stein answered herself with, "Well, in that case, what is the question?" and immediately lost consciousness and died. Alice B. Toklas died twenty-one years later and lies buried beside her in the cemetery at Pere-Lachaise in Paris.

Ernest Hemingway once famously said Gertrude Stein looked like a Roman emperor and, indeed, in the portraits by Pavel Tchelitchew and Jacques Lipchitz, she does rather resemble an ancient noble. Other friends marked her resemblance to a "Jewish

Buddha." Partially because she was an amazing-looking person and partially because her friends were mostly artists and other writers, she is a very well-documented individual. There are a multitude of portraits of her and many exceptional photographs by the likes of Cecil Beaton and Carl Van Vechten.

During her life, Gertrude Stein authored 600 novels, poems, essays, plays, opera librettos, and biographies. She influenced generations of writers after her; among those who claim her as inspiration are Edith Sitwell, Samuel Beckett, John Cage, and John Ashbery.

§ KATHERINE MANSFIELD *driven by duality*

At times, Katherine Mansfield's life story reads like a tale of two women. She is regarded as a great British writer, but she always felt like little Kathleen Beauchamp, the girl from New Zealand. She had a strict and conservative Victorian upbringing, but she was also bohemian. She had a husband and a "wife." Even her reasons for writing, as she explained them, were dual.

Her parents were conventional and proper; her father, Harold Beauchamp, was a Wellington banker, hardworking and ambitious. Daughter Kathleen was born in 1888.

Harold's wife Annie had a delicate constitution, and her sickliness convinced her she couldn't care for Kathleen on her own, so she moved her mother in to take care of her household and daughters. This was a boon for the child and her sisters, as they were given the affection her work-obsessed father and self-obsessed mother were unable to grant. When a son was born, the girls were sent off to several schools until 1903, when the family moved to London and

Kathleen enrolled in Queen's College for three years. She became an avid student, her favorite authors being the Brontë sisters, Elizabeth Robins, Leo Tolstoy, and Oscar Wilde. After her taste of the cosmopolitan city, Kathleen dreaded the return to New Zealand, but turned to writing as compensation. Her talent was recognized right away; her pieces were published in the local journal, *The Native Companion*. Her father was so impressed that she received payment for her monographs that he permitted her to go back to the London she loved.

She had a romantic correspondence with Tom Trowell, the son of her Wellington music instructor, but got engaged to Tom's twin brother Garnet. She also had a crush on a former schoolmate, Maata Mahupuka, a Maori heiress, and in college had met a motherless girl, Ida Constance Baker, with whom she formed a lifelong liaison. (Ida's father was the model for the overbearing patriarch in Mansfield's *The Daughters of the Late Colonel*.) Ida soon changed her name to L. M., Leslie Moore, and Kathleen began calling herself Katherine Mansfield.

Garnet Trowell's parents didn't approve of Katherine, and in a rash move, she married a man she had just met, George Bowden. She and L. M. went to the Registry Office for the civil ceremony, the bride clad all in black. That night, at the beginning of what should have been the honeymoon, she bolted and ran to L. M. for comfort. Mrs. Beauchamp got wind of her daughter's erratic antics and installed her in a German resort hotel where she was "treated" for her lesbian "affliction" with cold baths and spas. Katherine also recovered from a miscarriage that occurred at the hotel in Germany.

Throughout these romantic adventures, Mansfield wrote. Her first stories were published in A. R. Orage's *New Age;* those written from her sanitorium were published in a 1911 collection, *In a German Pension.* J. Middleton Murry, editor of a newly established review, *Rhythm,* immediately called her up when she submitted her story, "The Woman at the Store." In short order, Murry became a lodger and then lover of this writer, one year his senior. *Rhythm* was short-lived, but Mansfield continued to earn money for her writing to add to a tiny stipend from her father, and Murry wrote reviews and critical essays for pay.

With the onset of World War I, Mansfield's life and loves were pulled apart. Murry got an assignment for military intelligence, while L. M. became a machinist in an airplane factory. The Beauchamp family was devastated by the loss of their only son, who was "blown to bits" in France. *Prelude,* written in 1917, and *At the Bay,* written in 1921, are Katherine's ruminations about their time spent together in childhood, written in a style akin to stream of consciousness.

Her life in London saw Mansfield at the heart of a lively literary circle, with Virginia Woolf and D. H. Lawrence at the epicenter. Mansfield felt a strong kinship, a "sameness" with Lawrence. She saw his disposition as very much like hers and believed they were both attempting to express the erotic in words. She perceived Lawrence's attraction to her lover Murry as an attempt at a "blood brother-hood," and disapproved of his and his wife Frieda's incessant arguing in public—sudden, fierce outbursts that upset everyone around them. While Mansfield was oblivious to Lawrence's portrayal of her and Murry as Gudrun and Gerald in *Women in Love,* she avoided contact with him after he wrote her a nasty, accusing letter in 1920: "You revolt me, stewing in your consumption."

Katherine Mansfield's relationship to Virginia Woolf was equally crucial to her emotional and literary life. Woolf's upper-class, mannered background of comfortable wealth caused her occasionally to reprove Mansfield's unconventional lifestyle, referring to her as "common." But Woolf liked the younger writer's "inscrutable" intelligence more than she disliked her bohemianism. Mansfield looked up to Woolf and turned to her for comradely support, writing in a letter, "We have the same job, Virginia." Woolf's diaries contain an entry about Mansfield's stories as "the only writing I have ever been jealous of."

Mansfield's and Murry's relationship lasted her entire life, but, particularly after she developed tuberculosis, he was not to be relied on. Like Lawrence, he found her tuberculosis repulsive and seemed to feel more sorry for himself than her. Mansfield's satiric story, "The Man Without a Temperament," depicts his reaction to her illness perfectly. Murry withheld monetary as well as emotional support while she traveled in vain, searching for a place to get well. L. M. was her nurse, cook, valet, and rock, but the unfortunate circumstances of their togetherness eroded the relationship; Mansfield hated losing her independence, referred to L. M. as "The Albatross," and came to see her as a "hysterical ghoul."

Katherine Mansfield's health spiraled downward at a rapid pace but she refused to let it interfere with her writing. In 1918, she wrote *Bliss and Other Stories* while she suffered constant nausea, insomnia, night terrors, and chest pain; she could barely walk at times. *The Garden Party and Other Stories* was released to high praise; her crisp, precise prose and sharp dialogue won her comparisons to Anton Chekhov. At the end of her life, she was introduced to George Ivanovich Gurdjieff, founder of the Institute for the Harmonious Development of Man at Fountainebleau. Mansfield entered Gurdjieff's community unbeknownst to her friends; in an attempt to restore her health, she undertook the prescribed methods of movement and dance for "centering," living in a hayloft where she drank fresh milk, and lived above the dairy cows in a rustic room painted with pastoral scenes of flowers and animals. The night Murry came to visit her idyll, she hemorrhaged and died immediately.

> *One must be true to one's vision of life—in every*
> *single particular. . . . The only thing to do is to try*
> *from tonight to be stronger and better—to be whole.*

From the expurgated letters of Katherine Mansfield

---

§ THE WOMEN OF THE ROPE *a salon within a salon*

The influence of the enigmatic George Ivanovitch Gurdjieff, born George S. Georgiades in Armenia circa 1872, is global. Judging from the plethora of books and articles about him and the rapidly expanding popularity of the enneagram, an ancient wisdom he introduced to the West, today Gurdjieff's star is higher than ever. A shroud of mystery surrounded him, and details on his early life are thin. Purportedly, he spent his youth studying world religious traditions while traveling in India, Africa, Asia, and the Middle East before staking his claim on Europe and, later, America. Part of his mythology is a tale of stomach illness while in India, receiving several bullet wounds, passing though revolutions and wars, and long stays secreted away with assorted mystics, learning their recondite religious teachings.

Gurdjieff settled in Moscow in 1913 and taught there and in Petrograd, leaving for the Caucasus as the Russian Revolution swept across the territories in 1917. He had already attracted followers and founded his Institute for the Harmonious Development of Man two years later in what is now Tbilisi, in the state of Georgia, eventually relocating his center to Fontainebleau, France, in 1922. His utopian community was ascetic, the hard work and exercise regimen broken by an occasional feast where the dynamic Gurdjieff held court, lecturing on various themes. His core belief was that humans are "asleep" when they lead an ordinary life, but, through rigorous attention and work, one could "awaken," enjoying unprecedented awareness and energy. At these banquets, men and women from the community read from the master's writings and everyone physically able participated in ritual dance and movement to the musical compositions of Gurdjieff and Thomas deHartmann.

Everything about Gurdjieff is profoundly odd, but his relationship with the "Women of the Rope" is perhaps the strangest chapter of all. Paris in the 1930s and subsequent decades was a place of wild experimentation in art, literature, and social mores. The denizens of the Left Bank were especially open-minded and willing to embrace the avant-garde, even spiritually. A group of women well known in avant-garde literary circles became students of Gurdjeiff, calling themselves the "The Rope." The Rope included Georgette LeBland, a reputed soprano, accomplished writer of both prose and poetry and intimate of Jean Cocteau; Dorothy Caruso, the widow of the legendary Enrico Caruso, who became Margaret Anderson's lover after Georgette LeBland's death; Solita Solano, editor extraordinaire, whose secretarial notes from Gurdjieff's sessions provide the best-known records of the man and his methods; Alice Rohrer, a Pennsylvania farm girl who earned wealth from hatmaking, and, as purportedly the most emotional and least intellectual member, received the most attention; Kathryn Hulme, author of the award-winning *The Wild Place* and the novel that became an Audrey Hepburn star vehicle, *The Nun's Story;* Jane Heap, cofounder of the history-making *Little Review,* who went on to teach Gurdjieff's beliefs; Louise Davidson, actress and stage manager, who enjoyed the emotive aspect of the sessions; Elisabeth Gordon, the odd woman out, a conservative British spinster Gurdjieff had imprisoned as a "foreign national" during World War II; and Margaret Anderson, publisher with Heap of the *Little Review,* who dared first to publish Ezra Pound, T. S. Eliot, and James Joyce.

Gurdjieff lavished special attention on this lesbian sect of students, who met with him for private lessons. He prepared lavish meals for them at his apartment and treated them to expensive dinners in the finest Parisian bistros. One memorable evening included a very befuddled and cranky Frank Lloyd Wright. Gurdjieff kept them apart from his other groups and went so far as to give them intensive instruction that sometimes lasted for weeks. Gertrude Stein, their contemporary in both writerly pursuits and lesbianism, would have nothing to do with the mystic, but the others were set on gleaning as much arcane wisdom and insight as possible from their spiritual leader. He loved "shock tactics." Kathryn Hulme described in a letter to Jane Heap one bizarre session in which he took her to a bordello, insisting she choose one of the naked dancing women.

Gurdjieff taught that we all have an "inner animal." Each of the women of "The Rope" had a special name expressing this aspect of her nature with which he referred to her very affectionately. They began referring to each other as such, as well, in some cases, to the end of their lives:

Kathryn Hulme was Crocodile, pronounced "Krokodeel" by Gurdjieff.

Alice Rohrer, a former San Francisco milliner and companion to Hulme, was Boa Constrictor or "Theen One," who cried buckets during the teachings.

Solito Solano, editor and writer and longtime partner to Janet Flanner, was Canary. Initially resistant to Gurdjieff, after his death in 1949 she became the central figure of The Rope.

Margaret Anderson, arrested for first publishing James Joyce's *Ulysses* in *Little Review*, was Yakina, a Tibetan yak.

Noel Murphy, a later partner of Anderson after her break-up with Solita Solano, was Camel.

Gurdjieff's impact on The Rope was lasting; several remained lifelong believers and three wrote books about their time with the great spiritualist. As their moniker suggests, the women remained tied together by the experience.

> *Do not sit too long in the same place. You are responsible for what you have understood. Little steps for little feet. Suppress natural reaction and pay for it later. We never refuse in the Work. Animals are nature's experiments and embody all the emotions. A cat is all essence. Essence remembers. All that falls from the wagon is lost.*

> Gurdjieffian aphorisms from *The Notes of Jane Heap*

One of the leaders of the modernist literary movement, Virginia Woolf was born and raised in London to a family of letters; her father had an excellent reputation as a scholar and writer and authored the *The Dictionary of English Biography*. Her mother moved in artistic circles and hosted Edward Burne-Jones, William Holman Hunt, G. F. Watts, and stage actress Ellen Terry. Virginia was also accustomed to having literati visit her home; her parents entertained their noteworthy friends Henry James, Lord Tennyson, poet George Meredith, and writer-ambassador James Russell Lowell. In addition to her sister Vanessa, young Virginia Stephen had two natural brothers, Thoby and Adrian, a stepsister, Stella, and two stepbrothers, Gerald and George Duckworth. Though father Leslie Stephen was learned, he was not necessarily socially progressive, believing the girls needed to be educated at home.

Upon his death in 1905, the Stephens children shocked their relatives by closing the house they were raised in and relocating to Bloomsbury, a poorer neighborhood. There, they began to refashion life in accordance with their needs and interests. Thoby, a student at Cambridge and member of an underground organization, the Apostles, brought his friends over on Thursday evenings. These lively encounters quickly turned into a regular series of salons. This idyllic episode soon came to an end, however, when a group trip to Greece ended in Thoby dying of typhoid. A week later, still in mourning, Vanessa became engaged to Thoby's dear friend, Clive Bell, and set up a household in a Gordon Square row house. In 1907, Adrian and Virginia also moved to Fitzroy Square to a house formerly occupied by George Bernard Shaw. Brother and sister resumed holding salons in their new home, forming the true beginning of the Bloomsbury Group. Virginia keenly enjoyed the high-minded exchanges these evenings afforded her; they were often the highlight of her week.

She was an extremely sensitive person, given to occasional depressions and suicidal tendencies. She would go for long periods of time without eating, and is thought by some scholars to have been anorexic. An inveterate diarist, we know much about her state of mind, sexual advances by her stepbrothers, as well as her doubts, fears, and dreams. Her diaries also showed the beginnings of her "stream of consciousness" writing technique, an impressionistic, associative style reflecting the outer world through the inner world. She would also gossip about the various members of the salon and outer circles, the servants, and their extended family.

VIRGINIA WOOLF *Leader of the modernist literary movement and stream-of-consciousness stylist.*

Her salons were attended by a lively and brilliant group of accomplished poets, artists, and practicing homosexuals—Lytton Strachey, John Maynard Keynes, E. M. Forster, and Duncan Grant. At first Virginia was puzzled by their lack of interest in courting her, but she soon figured it out. Lytton Strachey developed an affection for Virginia and even went so far as to propose, confessing to his dear friend Leonard Woolf, at the time serving in Ceylon, "It would have been death if she had accepted me." He also had a much-publicized affair with a female artist, Dora Carrington, who committed suicide.

By 1910, the esteemed art critic Roger Fry had joined the group, later embarking on an affair with Vanessa Bell, whose marriage to Clive Bell was strained from raising two sons and from Clive's extramarital affairs. By 1911, Leonard Woolf returned from his India service and joined the Bloomsbury Group, now living communally in Fitzroy. Leonard and Virginia married, but soon after the honeymoon period he noticed her bouts of despondency. When she attempted suicide, a frightened, deeply concerned Leonard took on the role of caretaker, watching her eating habits, her menstrual patterns, and her moods. His vigilance worked fairly well in keeping her from sinking too low, but the depression she suffered was destined to return.

The members of the Bloomsbury Group worked steadily. Virginia, Leonard Woolf, and Forster began writing their first novels. Virginia also became very concerned with feminism and began doing volunteer work for suffragists. To the disgust of British art critics, Roger Fry held two Post-Impressionist exhibits followed by poetry and furniture-craft workshops. Vanessa Bell's skill in painting was developing rapidly, and her friendship with fellow painter Duncan Grant began to take a romantic bent. John Maynard Keynes was teaching his revolutionary economic theory at Cambridge, and Lytton was fast at work on his biographical survey, *Eminent Victorians.* By 1915, however, as their reputations were growing, the salon was held less frequently and the group gradually began drifting apart.

The Woolfs purchased a printing press and moved to Richmond to found Hogarth Press soon after the publication of Virginia's

VITA SACKVILLE-WEST *the love that cannot be spoken*

Born in Knole, Kent, in 1892, Victoria Mary Sackville is best remembered now as the subject of *Orlando*, Virginia Woolf's 1928 novel (which was made into a critically acclaimed film) about their love affair, told through the adventures of an androgynous and aristocratic heroine. Her father was the Third Baron Sackville and, as a child, Vita was afforded the very finest private education and tutors in her ancestral home, surrounded by a beautiful gardens and grounds. Her interest in writing began as a young girl with poetry, and she completed a history of her family and place, *Knole and the Sackville,* in 1922. She married diplomat and journalist Harold Nicolson, and they traveled extensively, resulting in her *Passenger to Teheran* and her travel fictions, *Heritage* and *The Dark Island*. Vita Sackville-West also write several fine biographies of Andrew Marvell, Aphra Behn, and of the saints Joan and Teresa of Avila. She became the subject of another book when her son Nigel Nicolson describes his parents' unusual marriage in *Portrait of a Marriage.*

debut novel, *The Voyage Out.* Hogarth Press published other seminal writers from this time, including Sigmund Freud, Katherine Mansfield, T. S. Eliot, and Gertrude Stein. Virginia Woolf was repulsed by James Joyce's work, however, and refused to publish him. Upon reading *Ulysses,* she recalled feeling as if "her very own pen had been seized from her hands so that someone might scrawl the word 'f' on the seat of a privy."

Vanessa Bell found a great old farmhouse in Sussex, Charleston, and invited the group to visit for parties, feasts, and weekend retreats. She threw Roger Fry over for the openly gay Duncan, with whom she had a baby, Angelica. Upon the baby's birth, the new father proclaimed that moment to be the end of their sexual relationship. One of Duncan Grant's lovers, David Garnett, wrote a letter to Lytton expressing a perverse urge to shock everyone, "I think of marrying it; when she is 20, I shall be 46—will it be scandalous?" The new parents were properly disgusted by this improper sentiment. (When Angelica grew up, she wrote the critically acclaimed book, *Deceived by Kindness.*)

Leonard Woolf eventually sold Hogarth Press to Harcourt Brace and carried on as Virginia's editor. Virginia wrote steadily and gained a serious following for her originality and singular style. Leonard Woolf remained vigilant in his self-appointed role as overseer of Virginia's physical and mental health, noting that the publication of each novel brought on one of her great depressions. His loyalty was unswerving, despite her affair with one of the writers they published, Vita Sackville-West, the subject of Virginia's novel *Orlando.*

In 1941, she was at the peak of her career—a critical success with books such as *To the Lighthouse* and *Mrs. Dalloway,* and mentor to a younger generation of writers, including Katherine Mansfield. But her fears for Leonard's and her own safety during World War II brought extreme anxiety; she was convinced they were in grave danger because of Leonard's Jewish heritage and fully expected to be captured and killed in a Nazi invasion. When she could bear it no more, she wrote a note to her beloved sister, Vanessa, and two notes to her husband: "I don't think two people could have been happier than we've been." She stuffed her pockets with heavy stones and walked into the river.

> *Against you I will fling myself, unvanquished and unyielding, O Death.*

> Bernard, from Virginia Woolf's *The Waves*

§ ZORA NEALE HURSTON *her eyes were watching God*

In recent decades, this American folklorist, novelist, and short story writer has received belated acclaim as a chronicler of African American culture. But she was also a major player in the Harlem Renaissance, an artistic and literary movement in the 1920s centered in Harlem, New York.

Born in 1891 (or 1901; Zora played loose with the dates), she was raised by a firebrand of a mother in Eatonville, Florida. After high school she attended Howard University in Atlanta, but soon moved on to Harlem in the early 1920s to become part of the burgeoning scene. The Harlem Renaissance was characterized by nonconformity to white literary standards and a celebration of blackness, particularly the discovery by educated, urban blacks of the vigor, beauty, and honesty of Harlem ghetto life. The leading writers in the movement, aside from Zora, were Langston Hughes, Jean Toomer, Countree Cullen, and Richard Wright. "In effect," writes *Benet's Readers Encyclopedia,* "the Renaissance group consisted of intellectuals in search of an identity: they stood some distance from their own people, yet felt alienated from mainstream American society."

In New York, Zora won a scholarship to Barnard College and later went on to obtain a graduate degree from Columbia, where she studied under the famous anthropologist Franz Boas. Franz encouraged her to study the folklore of the diaspora of African Americans, and that suggestion became her life's passion.

Her first collection of folk stories, *Mules and Men,* came from tales she collected in Alabama and Florida between 1929 and 1931. Its publication was greeted with great enthusiasm by the academic press, but, in a theme that would repeat itself throughout her life, she was criticized bitterly by some black reviewers for painting "too rosy" a picture of African American life and failing to include the degradation and shame of daily existence. (Zora's championing of black culture would get her into deeper trouble toward the end of her life, when she blasted the Supreme Court's school desegregation decision as an affront to the value of black institutions.)

Her most noted novel, *Their Eyes Were Watching God* (1937), is a poignant tale of a black woman's sexual and spiritual yearnings. Her autobiography *Dust Tracks on a Road* was published in 1942, and she also produced a series of short ethnographic films of rural black existence. The films currently reside in a University of California library and are occasionally exhibited.

Opinionated and single-minded, Hurston was married twice, but both marriages ended in divorce when she refused to give up traveling and collecting folk stories to be a stay-at-home wife. She fell into poverty in the 1950s as book sales fell off, and died alone and penniless in Fort Pierce, Florida, in 1960. She was buried in a segregated cemetery in a grave that remained unmarked until 1973, when writer Alice Walker erected at its site a stone marker reading: "Zora Neale Hurston, 1901–1960 A Genius of the South, Novelist, Folklorist, Anthropologist." Ironically, in the last twenty-five years, sales of Hurston's works have soared because of the well-publicized interest of others like Alice Walker and Oprah Winfrey, bringing her great acclaim and her estate great riches, both of which she was denied during her lifetime.

> *I do not belong to the sobbing school of Negrohood who hold down that nature somehow has given them a lowdown dirty deal and whose feelings are all hurt about it. Even in the helter-skelter skirmish that is my life, I have seen that the world is to the strong regardless of a little pigmentation more or less. I do not weep at the world—I am too busy sharpening my oyster knife.*

Zora Neale Hurston, from *How It Feels to Be Me*

DJUNA BARNES *enigma in exile*

While T. S. Eliot and James Joyce are widely heralded as having changed the landscape of twentieth-century literature, American Djuna Barnes, an important player in the same modernist movement, remains fairly obscure. Djuna was a published journalist and saw her plays, short stories, and both her novels greeted by critical praise. Her 1937 novel, *Nightwood,* is considered a classic, and met with a clamor of excitement from the literary world of that time. But when the *Little Review* pursued Barnes for an interview, she abjectly refused to talk about her life.

Born in upstate New York in 1892, Barnes was homeschooled by her grandmother, Zadel Barnes Budington, a published journalist and feminist who greatly influenced the young writer-to-be. Djuna's father, Wald Barnes, revered his strong-willed, intellectual mother and actually took her surname instead of his father's. Djuna's mother, Elizabeth Chappell Barnes, remains an elusive figure to biographers. The romantic view of Djuna's childhood is of artistic and rustic creativity à la Rousseau. The truth is not nearly so appealing; it seems that young Djuna was the recipient of both her grandmother's and her father's unwanted advances, and her father, with the apparent approval of her mother, "gave" Djuna as a mistress to the brother of his live-in mistress.

Nevertheless, the Barnes family still registered socially, and in their home Wald and Elizabeth Barnes hosted many of the great artists of their day, including Jack London and Franz Liszt. Djuna cherished this aspect of her family heritage; throughout her life, she counted among her friends many of the groundbreaking artists and writers of her day. When the Barnes family moved to a 105-acre farm on Long Island, Djuna wasted little time in becoming a part of New York City literary and art circles, studying for a time at Pratt Institute and the Art Students League. Here, she got her first taste of bohemian life and explored both her creativity and her sexuality.

Barnes made a splash almost immediately with a slender volume of poems and drawings, *The Book of Repulsive Women,* published as a chapbook in 1915. Her stories and poetry gained notice in a number of periodicals, and Djuna became a member of the Provincetown Players. Three of Djuna Barnes' plays were produced in a single season in the fall of 1919. By 1920, *McCall's* magazine hired her to do interviews of notables of the day and sent her to Europe.

Djuna Barnes pursued her *McCall's* assignment with her typical zeal, producing a memorable interview of filmmaker D. W. Griffith, animated tales of the "Jungle folk" at the circus, and an encounter with James Joyce, who ended up presenting her with the original manuscript for *Ulysses.* Her articles were steeped throughout with wit ("Nothing Amuses Coco Chanel after Midnight" was the title of one) and a disregard for convention that set her apart from her peers. She stayed in Paris for nearly twenty years as a correspondent for *Vanity Fair, Charm,* and the *New Yorker,* relishing the modernist scene.

Word of her beauty and appeal to both sexes quickly spread, and she enjoyed numerous affairs with both men and women. She married, briefly, writer Courtenay Lemon. She had a famously tempestuous affair with sculptor Thelma Wood, as well as flings with salonist and rival Natalie Barney, and Janet Heap, coeditor with Margaret Anderson of the *Little Review.* Djuna Barnes attracted friends as well as lovers: poet Mina Loy and affluent art patron Peggy Guggenheim both became quite close associates, and the extended salon included Janet Flanner, Dolly Wild, and Gertrude Stein. This circle of women came to be known as "The Academy of Women" and is now referred to as the literary women of "The Left Bank." Ever irreverent, Djuna Barnes later lampooned this salon scene in the satire *The Ladies Almanack.*

The Ladies Almanack was a skillfully and intricately woven web of puns and fables that also provided a fictionalized portrait of the expatriate writer Natalie Barney and the individuals in her salon. In it, Barnes staked out territory no one else dared dig into, taking an old-fashioned literary model and, though remaining faithful to form, adding dangerously modern plot twists. Though Djuna

Barnes attempted to dismiss *The Ladies Almanack* as a "slight satiric wigging" and "jollity" written "in an idle hour" for a "very special audience," namely lover Thelma Wood, she hand-colored fifty copies of the 1,050-copy printing and went as far as to take to the streets of Paris to hawk the book. Sylvia Beach helped Djuna a great deal when she began selling *The Ladies Almanack* in her shop, Shakespeare and Company. Though word-of-mouth, it became the talk of Paris, with everyone trying to guess who the "Ladies" really were. In *Ryder,* published in 1928, the central character was depicted as a "female Tom Jones" who swaggered throughout the tale with the comic arrogance of one who wants to rule the world. Both these books gained considerable notice for Barnes' high-spirited and highly skilled use of language, along with an accent upon female sexuality.

These same characteristics are true of Barnes' most important work, *Nightwood,* an experimental novel of an affair between two women and the musings of a Doctor O'Connor upon the two lovers. The manuscript racked up a record number of rejections, not even suffering, said biographer Andrew Fields, "the usual agonizing delays but shot in and out of the publishers' offices as though it were being ejected from a greased revolving door in an old silent movie."

Finally, the manuscript made its way into the hands of T. S. Eliot, who, with Barnes' permission, edited the novel as he saw fit, came up with the title, and wrote the introduction, acclaiming it as "so good a novel that only sensibilities trained on poetry can wholly appreciate it." His high praise cemented the importance of the book and catapulted Djuna Barnes into the rarefied air of "writers who matter." Some feminist literary historians, however, believe that the relationship between Barnes and Eliot may have not been so benign, focusing on the now-controversial editing of *Nightwood,* a slender 50,000 words in final published form, 15,000 words less than the version Barnes sent to Eliot, and immensely shorter than the original 190,000. According to scholar Shari Benstock, Eliot reduced the manuscript by two-thirds and cut "among other things—scenes that expressed explicate lesbian rage and virulent anticlerical sentiment."

In the mid-1930s, Barnes suffered a series of breakdowns. In 1939, one year before the Occupation of Paris in World War II, Peggy Guggenheim paid her passage to New York. Barnes lived out the rest of her life in hiding, more than forty years of seclusion broken by an occasional quarrel, illness, or interruption by her neighbor, fellow poet e. e. cummings, yelling out his window, "Are ya still alive, Djuna?" Her impoverished isolation and descent into depression, drugs, drinking, and dementia was relieved slightly by Samuel Beckett, Peggy Guggenheim, and Natalie Barney, who, along with the National Endowment for the Arts, subsidized her scanty income. Barnes' avoidance of life outside her apartment door has, sadly, resulted in her obscurity. A handful of writers including Anaïs

Nin, Isak Dinesen, Truman Capote, and John Hawkes claimed Barnes as a major influence on their own work. Along with Nathaniel West, best remembered for *The Day of the Locust*, Djuna Barnes has been identified as an innovator of black comedy, and, according to critic Donald J. Greiner, *Nightwood* "stands our among post-World War I American novels as one of the first notable experiments with a type of comedy that makes the reader want to lean forward and laugh with terror."

> *Red cheeks. Auburn hair. Gray eyes, ever sparkling*
> *with delight and mischief. Fantastic earrings in her*
> *ears, picturesquely dressed, ever ready to liveand to*
> *be merry: that's the real Djuna as she walks down*
> *Fifth Avenue or sips her black coffee, a cigarette in*
> *hand, in the Cafe Lafayette. Her morbidity is not a*
> *pose. It is as sincere as she is herself.*

Guido Bruno, from an interview with Djuna Barnes

---

§ H. D (HILDA DOOLITTLE) *the poet's poet*

References to H. D. come up most frequently when modern poets are asked to name their influences. In an odd twist of time and fate, her reputation is ascending, while her fellow poet and mate Ezra Pound is finding less favor in the canonical memory. Previously, she was best remembered for a few poems named by Pound as foundation stones of the modernist movement he called Imagism.

The only daughter in a family of five sons, Hilda Doolittle was born in 1886, was raised for her first eight years in Bethlehem,

Pennsylvania, a community of German immigrants, and then moved to Philadelphia. Her family was socially prominent; her father, Charles Doolittle, was a professor. Hilda's mother, Helen Wolle Doolittle, was a member of the Moravian brotherhood, a rare mystical Hussite sect of Protestantism based on a doctrine of wisdom received directly and bodily from God. H. D. credits this "gift" of spirit and vision passed down generationally among Moravians as an important part of what informed her poetry. Hilda attended the Gordon School, later the Friends Central School, and Bryn Mawr.

A sensitive young woman, she had difficulty living away from home and, after failing English, left college and suffered a breakdown. H. D.'s fictionalized autobiography *HERmoine*, written in 1923 and unpublished until 1981, examines this period in terms of the relationship between H. D. and her fiancée, Ezra Pound, whom she had met at college, and her beloved friend Frances Gregg. William Carlos Williams admired Hilda as a great beauty, which Pound also celebrated in his *Is-Hilda Book*. In 1911, Hilda, Frances, and chaperone Mrs. Gregg went abroad, and Hilda's extended expatriation began with her reunion with Ezra Pound in London.

H. D. and Pound found like minds in D. H. Lawrence, William Butler Yeats, May Sinclair, and Richard Aldington. Hilda took the excellent advice of her lover and submitted poems to *Poetry* magazine, edited by Harriet Monroe. Her distinct pseudonym began, somewhat accidentally, when Ezra Pound signed Hilda Doolittle's poems "H. D. Imagiste" in August 1912 in the British Museum's tea room. Pound praised the qualities he saw in H. D.'s verse as essential in Imagist poetry—musical rhythm, minimalism, direct approach of the poetry subject. Her first collection, *Sea Garden*, was published in 1916. While their poetic sympathies were perfectly matched, H. D. began to strain against Pound's intransigence and his seeming inability to remain faithful to her. Another mentor took his place both in H. D.'s life and at the landmark literary periodical, *The Egoist* (originally, *The New Freewoman*): Richard Aldington. Under his influence as a translator, H. D. began to study Greek lyrics, French symbolism, and the romances of medieval troubadours. In 1913, H. D. married her new mentor.

Women who love books too much

H. D. and her husband made an important new friend in Amy Lowell, a moneyed American poet who published their work in three anthologies and a book of literary criticism in which she commended both Imagism and, in particular, H. D.'s poetry. D. H. and Frieda Lawrence formed a closer bond with the pair, and this foursome shared a great intimacy surrounded by swirling speculation. While H. D. based characters in *Pilate's Wife* and *Bid Me to Live* on the Lawrences, D. H. Lawrence memorialized H. D. as his bohemian character Julia in *Aaron's Rod*.

After the invention of the printing press in the fifteenth century, women were often at the helm of these new machines. The most famous was Parisian Yolande Bonhomme, who, as both publisher and printer, churned out more than 200 titles in thirty years between 1500 and 1600.

H. D. and D. H. shared many things in common, including a loathing for the war that began on the eve of their meeting and a love for esoterica, myth, and the natural world. Their differences were difficult to ignore; H. D. often found Lawrence to be smugly superior and patriarchal, and, it is implied in *Bid Me to Live,* she resented it when he withdrew from a sexual relationship with her.

When World War I broke out in 1915, H. D. suffered a miscarriage that she always associated with the hostilities. Two years later, the Lawrences moved into H. D.'s flat in London, Richard Aldington began training as an army officer and, simultaneously, embarked on an affair with a friend of H. D.'s. In 1918, Aldington was sent to the front lines of battle in France, and H. D.'s brother Gilbert died in combat. This tragedy was followed almost immediately by the death of H. D.'s father; soon after she became pregnant after taking a trip with music critic Cecil Gray. A bout with double pneumonia nearly cost H. D. her own life and that of her unborn child. H. D. claimed they were saved by a twenty-four-year-old woman, Winifred Ellerman, or "Bryher," who mothered the dangerously ill poet through her sickness.

H. D. retells this very difficult period in her life in her novel *Palimpset.* Bryher was born out of wedlock to an enormously wealthy and powerful British shipping magnate; her main ambition in life was to write adventure novels about boys. She was a huge fan of H. D.'s, even going so far as to memorize *Sea Garden.* Bryher paid for the publication of *Hymen* in 1921, paid H. D.'s bills, and adopted H. D.'s daughter, Perdita. In 1919, Bryher took them to Greece, realizing a lifelong dream of H. D.'s to go to the source of inspiration, the home of the muses, as it were. Here, H. D. experienced her first psychic vision, which she later described as "writing on the wall." It included images of a tripod, a still-helmeted dead soldier, and Niké, the goddess of victory. Bryher took over for H. D. when she became too fatigued and "channeled" the final vision of winged Niké mating with Helios, the God of the Sun. Together, the women believed they had seen through to an archetypal narrative beyond space and time, a timeless story of female rebirth that recurred in H. D.'s poetry ever after. This auspicious journey led them on further pilgrimages to Paris, Egypt, and America in search of more victorious visions.

This beatific spate of creativity was followed by a dry spell that left H. D. anxious about what she feared was her decline, leading her to seek analysis with Sigmund Freud, as depicted in her critically acclaimed impressionist *Tribute to Freud,* first published in 1944. Freud's theories regarding H. D. varied from an unresolved attachment to her mother to penis envy in her relationships with the male poets in her life. H. D. countered this with her own belief that she was more spiritually attuned and intuitive than Freud was able to allow with his rigid psychoanalysis.

H. D.'s subsequent works were overtly feminist. She composed two epics about war, *Trilogy* and *Helen in Egypt,* and later wrote a meditation on the role of the sacred prostitute Mary Magdalene in Christ's life. After World War II, H. D. underwent a breakdown and moved from London to Switzerland, but continued to work on *Hermetic Definition,* published finally in 1972.

H. D. delved more deeply into mysticism and the occult, working with Tarot cards, astrology, and Moravian ritual. She had several more affairs, including ones with Sir Hugh Carswell Dowding, Chief Air Marshall of the Royal Air Force Fighter Command, and Haitian journalist Lionel Durand, after she turned seventy. In 1960, H. D. came to America one last time to accept the Award of Merit Medal for Poetry from the American Academy of Arts and Letters. Poets like Denise Levertov and Robert Duncan claim her as an influence, but toward the end of her life, H. D. refuted the notion that she was influenced by Pound and Lawrence, counting them as co-creators only. in her poetry, H. D. was in search of "what men say not" and proclaimed "the mother is the Muse, the Creator."

> *Take care, do not know me*
> *shun me; for this reality*
> *is infectious—ecstasy!*

> H. D.

§ SIMONE DE BEAUVOIR *on her own terms*

Existentialist writer Simone de Beauvoir was the founder of the feminist movement in France. Her book, *The Second Sex,* immediately

took a place of importance in the feminist canon upon its publication in 1949 and established Beauvoir's reputation as a first-rate thinker. Although her brutally honest examination of the condition of women in the first half of the twentieth century shocked some delicate sensibilities, others were gratified to have someone tell the truth of women's experience as "relative beings."

Born in 1908 to what she characterized as "bourgeois" parents, she met the philosopher Jean-Paul Sartre in her early twenties in a salon study group at Paris' famed university, the Sorbonne. They recognized each other as soulmates immediately and stayed together for fifty-one years in a highly unorthodox partnership, wherein they left openings for "contingent loves" so as not to limit their capacity for enriching experience. She eschewed motherhood and all forms of domesticity; the duo prefered cafés for all their meals. They lived together only very briefly during

SIMONE DE BEAUVOIR *France's Existentialist par excellance*

THE MABEL DODGE SALON

Anybody who was anybody in the literary and art worlds of the early twentieth century hung out at Mabel's salon, among them: D. H. Lawrence, Gertrude Stein, Alice B. Toklas, Andrew Dassburg, Georgia O'Keeffe, Leon Gaspard, Ansel Adams, and Robinson Jeffers. Beginning in New York's Greenwich Village after a stint in a Medici villa in Florence, Mabel Dodge worked for her vision of a "New World Plan" to bring the world's greatest thinkers, writers, artists, musicians, and social reformers together to whet each other's minds and create a second renaissance. Lois Palken Rudnick, a historian specializing in this era, says this about Mabel: "When she came back to the States, she landed in New York City amidst America's first great social and political revolution. She became one of the rebels of Greenwich Village and was involved with the Armory Show, the first show of post-impressionist art to come to the states. She supported anarchists and socialists and their projects, like Emma Goldman and Margaret Sanger.... She was an artist of life." Dodge was also a member of the Heterodoxy Club, a pioneering feminist group that functioned as a "salon within a salon."

World War II and had difficulty protecting their privacy as word of the trendy new philosophy they espoused spread and their international prestige heightened.

While Sartre is generally credited as the creator of existentialism, Beauvoir and the circle of leftist intellectuals that surrounded them were intricately involved in defining the movement. Her treatise *Existentialism and the Wisdom of the Ages* postulates the human condition as neutral, neither inherently good nor evil: "[The individual] is nothing at first," she theorized, "it is up to him to make himself good or bad depending upon whether he assumes his freedom or denies it."

Beauvoir's first literary efforts were fictional. In 1943's *She Came to Stay,* she fictionalizes the story of Sartre's youthful protégé Olga Kosakiewicz, who entered into a triangular living relationship with the two French intellectuals. Next, she tackled the male point of view in her epic treatment of death, *All Men Are Mortal,* a novel whose central character was an immortal she tracked for seven centuries. In 1954, after the success of *The Second Sex,* Beauvoir returned to fiction with *The Mandarins,* a novelization of the splintered and disenchanted French intelligentsia, including thinly disguised portrayals of Sartre, Albert Camus, and Nelson Algren, among others, which won the illustrious Goncourt Prize.

She continued to write and publish, creating a weighty body of work. Her penetrating mind is perhaps most evident in the series of five memoirs she wrote, the most famous of which is the first, *Memoirs of a Dutiful Daughter.* She outlived Sartre and died on a Paris summer day in 1986 after a long and thoughtful life, leaving a legacy of significant contributions to gender and identity issues as well as philosophy and literature.

The first novel, The Tale of Genji, *was written around 1010 by an aristocratic Japanese woman known now to the world as Lady Murasaki (the name of the heroine of her novel) so that she and the women of the Japanese Court would have something to read. Before this, reading was the province of men in Japan.*

One is not born a woman, one becomes a woman.

The first line of Simone de Beauvoir's *The Second Sex*

The very name of this writer rolls trippingly off the tongue, Dor-o-thy—ending with two sonorous and sharp syllables—Par-ker—very deliberate syllables, at that. Immediately, a picture forms of high style and hard drinks at the Algonquin Hotel. Deadly wit and comic timing aside, all was not glamour for the highly readable and addictively quotable character. Dorothy's life was hard.

A West End, New Jersey, girl, Dorothy Rothschild's mother was Scottish and her father was Jewish. Born in 1893, her mother passed away when Dorothy was quite young. She was raised by her father, a garment manufacturer, and her stepmother, who took up residence in New York's Upper West Side and sent her to a convent school and later, Miss Dana's School, an upper-crust girls' school in Morristown, New Jersey. Dorothy regarded her parents as tyrants, seething alternately with fear of them and loathing for them.

She escaped into writing and discovered she had a way with words. Her first job was writing photograph captions for *Vogue*, where she charmed readers and editors alike with her perfect bon mots; "Brevity is the soul of Lingerie" for undergarments was one such nugget. In 1917, Dorothy met and married Wall Street businessman Edwin Pond Parker II. The marriage was rocky, and the young Mrs. Parker despaired over an abortion in 1923 and made her first attempt at suicide. Things completely fell apart when Edwin Parker returned from his tour of duty in World War I, and the couple divorced in 1928.

During this time, Dorothy's sense of drama gained her employment as theater critic for the magazines *Ainslee's* and *Vanity Fair*. Her first volume of poetry, *Enough Rope,* was published in 1926 and was a triumph. She was chummy with Harold Ross, Robert Sherwood, and Robert Benchley, and was soon ensconced at the Algonquin Hotel's Round Table lunches. Ross and she were utterly simpatico, and he saw her potential to add punch to his new magazine, the *New Yorker*. Ross proved prescient; Dorothy Parker's columns, reviews, and stories helped shape the landmark magazine. Parker quit *Vanity Fair* immediately and basked in the accolades for her intelligent humor and satiric edge.

While popular success was hers, some critics sharpened their pens to match wits with hers and dismissed her writing as insubstantial. Parker was very unhappy personally and had a serious of messy affairs, drank a lot, and sank into depression. She attempted suicide three times in the '20s, but managed to keep writing even during the desolation. Three more books, *Sunset Gun, Death and Taxes,* and *Not So Deep as a Well* were greeted with plaudits.

Her next marriage, to fellow writer Alan Campbell, was even less stable than her first. Campbell was bisexual and eleven years younger than Dorothy Parker. The two worked on screenplays together, collaborating on

DOROTHY PARKER *her rapier wit gave New York its edge*

the fantastic *A Star Is Born*. While marriage wasn't the right fit, there was a strong connection, and they remarried, split up, and got back together several times.

Dorothy Parker's political views were progressive. She was very vocal in her protest of the execution of accused anarchists Sacco and Vanzetti, and she spoke out against fascism during the Spanish Civil War. Hollywood didn't approve of this political activism, and both Dorothy Parker and Alan Campbell were summarily blacklisted in the 1940s, costing them their livelihood of $5,000 a week.

Parker's moods swung with the ups and downs of the marriage until Campbell died in 1963. A dispirited Dorothy Parker then spent her remaining years drowning her insecurities in drink. Not unlike the lonely women who inhabited her stories, Parker lived an unconventional life, taking risks and expressing her views even at great personal cost. More than thirty years after her passing, her sensibility still shapes our culture. A truly original mind, she never hesitated to speak it.

> *Guns aren't lawful; Nooses give; Gas smells awful;*
> *you might as well live.*
>
> Dorothy Parker, from "Resume"

seven
Women Whose Books Are Loved Too Much

Adored Authors

THIS IS A deeply subjective subject, and could, perhaps should, be an entire book. Maybe you hold an undying loyalty to Louisa May Alcott, have read *Little Women* countless times, going though tons of tissue every time you read about Beth dying. Perhaps you have remained enthralled by Jane Austen and know that you could have portrayed Emma much more convincingly than did Gwyneth Paltrow. Chances are, you have waxed evangelical about the *Divine Secrets of the Ya-Ya Sisterhood,* even going so far as to dress up, Vivi-style, savoring juicy quotes over a Singapore Sling at a barbecue. Maybe you are guilty of re-reading your son's *Harry Potter* books in secret.

Why do certain books and certain writers inspire such devotion? Maybe it is best not to overanalyze this but simply to indulge and enjoy. Some books should absolutely be read again and again, each time uncovering something new to enjoy. These are not guilty pleasures; these are sacred rites. If Anne Rice's baroque adventures of the undead send shivers up your spine each time, then by all means keep reading. Rice reports that her home in the garden district of New Orleans has become a pilgrimage shrine, and that it is fine with her. I confess I have a photo of myself in a leopard-print raincoat clutching a copy of *Interview with a Vampire* in front of her gothic manse.

Among my other literary journeys, I tracked down Gertrude Stein's "no there there" childhood home in a forgotten part of Oakland, California, my heart nearly stopping when I saw a huge old rose bush in spectacular full bloom, imagining that was the primordial plant that inspired her immortal "A rose is a rose is a rose" line. That endeavor merely took six months and a furtive favor from a city employee who tracked down the property records. But, I couldn't help myself. I had read her stunning and confounding *How to Write* and a biography of her life with Alice B. Toklas. I felt driven to connect with her in some way, but my budget didn't allow for a trip to Paris, the city of her life, love, and interment. Alice Walker's journey to the backwaters of Florida to find Zora Neale Hurston's unmarked grave is a testament to her love of books and to the legacy of a great and, until then, nearly forgotten writer. Many have trekked to the place where Anne Frank hid behind the walls, writing in the diary that, years after her death, sparkles with the intelligence and spirit of a girl who refused to be doomed.

This section is intended as a tribute to the women whose books incite such fervency and allegiance. Long may their immortal tomes be relished and read, again and again.

Bibliophile Ruth M. Baldwin amassed a collection of over 100,000 nine-teenth- and twentieth-century children's books, which she donated to the University of Florida. But even after the collection was installed there, she controlled access to the books with "an iron hand," recalled a librarian. She set up a desk at the door, "and if she didn't think your reason for wanting to see something was good enough, you were gone."

§ JANE AUSTEN   *mannered master*

It is hard to believe that Jane Austen, today beloved by readers every-where and regarded as one of the true masters of the English novel, received little critical or popular attention during her lifetime.

Indeed she spent twenty-five years writing novels—gems that read-ers now recognize as masterpieces of irony, morality, and vivid char-acterizations—that were not even published under her name. Many of her novels center on finding husbands for marriageable daugh-ters, a theme familiar to Jane from her own life.

Born in Hampshire, England, in 1775, she was the seventh child of the Reverend George Austen and his wife, Cassandra. While he had an inherited income that he supplemented by tutoring, his brood of eight children cost a pretty penny; resources were tight. And, like Jane's character Mr. Bennet in *Pride and Prejudice,* he didn't have much to give his two daughters to marry on. Jane was edu-cated at home, aside from a short stint at a boarding school. At home she read prodigiously (her father had a library of 500 books), played the piano, and drew.

As a young adult, she attended many social events, where she trained her witty eye on the com-ings and goings of the people of her class. Her observations would later inform her novels, including *Northanger Abbey, Persuasion* (both 1818), *Sense and Sensibility* (1811), *Mansfield Park* (1814), and *Emma* (1816). She had a flirtation with Tomas Lefroy in 1795, but this didn't come to anything

JANE AUSTEN *Hollywood's favorite "new screenwriter."*

Not surprisingly, there exist a number of Jane Austen Web sites, including the scholarly one by the Jane Austen Society of North America ("a serious but not stuffy group," they maintain) at www.jasna.org, and my personal favorite at www.pemberley.com, which serves us such tasty items as the Jane Austen Punishments List, which includes: relationship advice from Lady Russell; a visit to a library with Miss Bate; a night of babysitting Lady Middleton's children; one day of nursing Mary Musgrove through one of her illnesses; and a weekend in Reno or Las Vegas with Mr. Darcy.

because he couldn't afford to marry her. The family moved to Bath in 1801, and Jane had to go with them—unmarried daughters did *not* live away from home, no matter their age. Here the twenty-seven-year-old apparently fell in love with a mysterious suitor who promised to marry her but died before they could exchange vows. Critics have speculated that she used this personal sorrow to great effect in *Persuasion*. In 1805, her father died, and, like the characters in *Pride and Prejudice*, she, her sister, and her mother were left in extreme circumstances, relying on the meager help of her brothers. One of the brothers provided a house for the three, and they moved to Chawton.

During all this she was writing and even managed to sell *Northanger Abbey* to a publisher for ten pounds. (They didn't publish it, however, until after her death, fourteen years later.) Refusing to be discouraged, she continued writing. Her first published novel, *Sense and Sensibility*, appeared anonymously ("By a Lady"), and at first only her family knew it was she who had written it. After *Pride and Prejudice* appeared, even though it too was anonymous, outsiders began to ascertain that she was the author. Even though her books began to appear regularly, she made virtually no money. Her publishers forced her to pay for her own reprints and she sold the copyright to *Pride and Prejudice* for a small lump sum and therefore received no royalties.

By 1816, she was suffering from ill health, ground down by money troubles. One of her brothers who had helped support her went bankrupt and another lost a large sum. She died in 1817 at age forty. It was only after her death that her books began to identify their author. Today, her novels continue to attract widespread attention, in part due to the series of films that have brought new readers to this beloved author

Those who do not complain are never pitied.

Jane Austen

CHRISTINA FOYLE *the lady who lunched*

Christina Foyle was born into the book business. She was the child of William, who in 1904 founded with his brother one of the most famous bookstores of all time: Foyle's in London. The store was renowned for its layout—books were filed by publisher rather than author. When Christina was seventeen, she joined the store and began hosting the Foyle's literary luncheons, which brought readers together with the great thinkers and writers of the day, and continued until her death in 1999. During the seven decades she presided over the lunches, she met many of the century's leading writers and politicians, including George Bernard Shaw, Bertrand Russell, and J. B. Priestley.

§ MARY WEBB AND IVY COMPTON-BURNETT *revivals of the fittest*

Diehard fans of all kinds of authors are filling the Internet with their passions, resulting in revivals of a number of writers. Two such women are Britain's Mary Webb and Ivy Compton-Burnett. Webb (1881–1927) is the author of the mystical novels *Precious Bane* (which won the 1924 Prix Femina Vie Heureuse) and *Gone to Earth,* among others. Hailed as a genius by Rebecca West, she remains relatively unknown today, although after her death, Britain's Prime Minister Stanley Baldwin acclaimed her work.

A society dedicated to Webb, founded in 1972, is spreading the word. It holds a summer school, has a journal and an e-mail discussion group, and rotates the job of putting fresh flowers on her grave. Devotees can find it online at **www.wlv.ac.uk/~me1927/mwebb.html**.

Ivy Compton-Burnett is another figure worthy of booklovers' attention. Born in 1884, she began writing in her forties and penned a series of cool, witty, and ironic novels that sold well through World War II. But unlike her contemporaries, Virginia Woolf, D. H. Lawrence, and James Joyce, she is not widely read these days, which is a shame, for she is hailed by critics. In 1996, A. N. Wilson listed in the *Evening Standard* the 100 books that everyone should read, and Ivy's *More Women Than Men* came right after *Pride and Prejudice* among only twenty English novels.

When her first novel, *Pastors and Masters,* appeared, the *New Statesman* proclaimed, "It is astonishing, amazing. It is like nothing else in the world. It is a work of genius." She was well regarded in avant-garde circles, her work hailed as "the closest it was possible to come to post-impressionism in fiction," writes her biographer

Women Whose Books Are Loved Too Much
Adored Authors

215

Hilary Spurling. Though avant-garde as a writer, she "dressed and behaved more like a Victorian governess," says Spurling, using Victorian trappings as a "protective cover behind which her penetrating subversive intelligence might operate unsuspected, freely and without constraints."

If you would like to join in on the Compton-Burnett revival, go to **www.brightlightsfilm.com/ivy/ivyon.html**.

My novels are hard not to put down.

Ivy Compton-Burnett, on her work

§ ANNE FRANK *behind the attic wall*

If Anne Frank had lived, what would she think of the fact that her diary of the two years her family spent in hiding from the Nazis would go on to become not only a classic of war literature, but one of the most widely read and loved books of all time? *The Diary of Anne Frank* is now handed down from one generation to the next, and reading the records of Anne's emotions has become a rite of passage for the teens of today. It has been translated into more than fifty languages, made into a play and a movie; a new English version, published in 1995, restored one-third more material that was cut out of the original by her father.

Why such popularity? Anne Frank's diary shows the human face of an inhuman war while it records a young girl's emotional growth with great insight. When she passed through the walls behind the bookcases into the secret rooms of the attic in Amsterdam, she left her real life behind. At thirteen, Anne became a prisoner and fugitive at once. Torn from her friends at the onset of her teens, she poured her heart into the diary she called "Kitty," her imaginary a friend and confessor. It's an intense experience for the reader who knows what Anne couldn't know—she wouldn't survive. Anne believed she would make it and shares her hopes and wishes for the children she will one day have. She died in the concentration camp at Bergen-Belsen at sixteen.

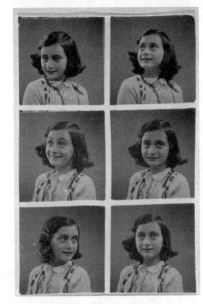

There is heartbreak also in the realization of what a gift for writing Anne had—it is almost unfathomable that some of the passages were written by an adolescent. Her honesty about her feelings, not all of them noble, is the quality that makes Anne's diary eternal. Caged in a hidden world, Anne showed us

ANNE FRANK *The world's most read and beloved diarist.*

that a life of the mind could be full, no matter what the circumstances. For her courage and optimism, Anne Frank will always be beloved.

> *The best remedy for those who are afraid, lonely, or unhappy is to go outside, somewhere where they can be quite alone with the heavens, nature, and God. . . . I firmly believe that nature brings solace in all troubles.*

> Anne Frank

§ MARJORIE KINNAN RAWLINGS
life in the backwoods

What child has not read—and loved—*The Yearling*, Marjorie Kinnan Rawlings' sensitive portrayal of life in the Florida Everglades? It is a schoolroom classic.

Born in 1896, as a girl Marjorie used to play "Story Lady" in Washington, D.C., making up stories to tell the boys from her neighborhood. As an adult, she was a syndicated journalist before she and her husband moved to Cross Creek, Florida. There she fell in love with the unique people of Southern Florida and their heart in the face of hardship, poverty, and starvation, which she immortalized in her memoir *Cross Creek.*

Through her writings, Rawlings helped focus the nation's attention on an area previously disregarded as a "wasteland." Through her O'Henry Award-winning short stories like "Gal Young Un" and "The Black Secret" and her novels—*South Moon Under, The Sojourner,* and *The Yearling*—readers came to appreciate the beauty of this unique ecosystem.

The Yearling shows Rawlings at the top of her craft. A beautifully rendered story and sense of place, the book won a Pulitzer Prize in 1939. *The Yearling* was

MARJORIE KINNAN RAWLINGS *Author of* The Yearling *and chronicler of the unique people and region of the Florida Everglades.*

made into a film that received both critical and popular acclaim, cementing Rawlings' spot in the list of authors of most beloved books.

Recently Rawlings has come in for a good deal of renewed attention. In 1999, a book of her voluminous correspondence with her editor Max Perkins was published by the University Press of Florida, and Rawlings' maid, Idella Parker, published her autobiography, full of reminiscences of the hard-living writer who smoked nearly six packs of cigarettes a day. In *Max and Marjorie,* Rawlings' and Perkins' remarkable epistolary relationship is revealed. Perkins was her literary champion, offering editorial opinion, a week-by-week critique of her work, and gossip about the other writers he shepherded, particularly Ernest Hemingway, F. Scott Fitzgerald, and Thomas Wolfe.

§ AGATHA CHRISTIE *first lady of crime*

Another writer with a devoted following is Agatha Christie, whom many fans think of as their cherished Miss Marple. She was born in 1890 into comfortable circumstances to an upper-class family, surrounded by books, notably those of Sherlock Holmes. She aroused public interest when she was at the center of a mystery of her own as a young woman. She disappeared and then reemerged, never explaining her whereabouts. (This incident recently became the subject of a novel.)

At the age of thirty, her first book, *The Mysterious Affair at Styles,* was published. This was not only Christie's debut, but also the first appearance of Hercule Poirot, one of her detective characters. Poirot would go on to incite fierce loyalty from her readers, though the author herself grew rather tired of him and the droves of fan letters she received for him. "Little they know, I can't bear him now," she once remarked. The clever spinster, Miss Marple, actually didn't enter the literary scene until ten years later, in 1930, with the release of *The Murder at the Vicarage.*

Christie had invented several other sleuths before her death in 1976, but none so popular as these two key figures. While she sometimes felt confined to the genre (penning more than eighty mysteries) and was generally discouraged by her publishers and fans from writing anything else, she did manage to write romantic fiction under the *nom de plume* Mary Westmacott. Several of her stories were adapted to the theater, including *Mousetrap,* which for many years held the title of the longest-running play in theater history. Today she remains the most famous author of detective fiction, and the most widely translated author in English, even inciting a fervent fan-base in Communist Russia.

But of course, detective stories supported me and my daughter for years, and they had to be written.

Agatha Christie

AGATHA CHRISTIE *Queen of the murder mystery, unbeknownst to many she authored romance fiction under the pseudonym Mary Westmacott.*

§ MARGARET MITCHELL *fame in "the wind"*

The fiery, red-headed, Irish Southern belle, whose family typified the antebellum South, went through a terrible war, saw her hometown of Atlanta burned in an uncontrollable conflagration, and lived to see the day when its streets were filled with soldiers. No, it wasn't Scarlett O'Hara, but her creator and alter ego, whose family were central characters in the history of Georgia.

Born in 1900, Margaret Mitchell came of age during the great mobilization of World War I. Her mother was feminist Maybelle Mitchell, a noted suffragist and founder of the Atlanta Women's Study Club. "Nothing infuriated her so much," reported Margaret later, "as the complacent attitude of other ladies who felt they should let the gentlemen do the voting." She immortalized Mama in her famous novel, modeling the character of Rhett Butler after the tough-minded Maybelle.

A former flapper (using her maiden name in a manner very uncharacteristic of genteel southern ladies in the early decades of the century), Margaret began writing her epic novel in 1926, after a serious ankle injury ended her brief career as a columnist for the *Atlanta Journal*. Never intended for publication, *Gone with the Wind* was instead viewed by Margaret as a very private exercise where she could weave together many of the stories that surrounded her. The manuscript evolved over a period of ten years into a massive cluttered stack of disjointed papers. She rarely spoke about it to anyone, although after awhile the existence of this huge pile of words became common knowledge among her friends, one of whom was MacMillan editor Harold Latham. In a 1935 visit to Atlanta, Latham asked Margaret if he could take a look at it.

Impulsively, and, in retrospect, surprisingly, for someone who considered herself a poor writer and was extremely private about her writing, Margaret bundled up the huge stack of handwritten pages and dumped them onto his lap. Almost immediately she had second thoughts, and when Latham got back to New York, he found a telegram informing him that she had changed her mind and to send the manuscript back. By then, he had already become ensnared in the saga (even though at the time it lacked a first chapter and any semblance of order).

The rest, as they say, is history. *Gone with the Wind* was published in 1936. This huge (over 1,000 pages) romantic saga of struggle and perseverance immediately captured the imagination of the Depression-battered public, becoming a monumental bestseller. It was also the last book Margaret Mitchell would write (she had previously written parts of two novellas, *Pansy Hamilton Flapper Heroine* and *Ropa Carmagin,* but both remained unpublished and were destroyed after her death by her family). In 1996, *Lost Laysen*, another lost novella, was published by her estate, but it failed to capture the same attention as her greatest work.

The sheer scope of impact that *Gone with the Wind* has made on the American cultural landscape is breathtaking. In many respects, due to its incredibly evocative description of the antebellum South, it has come to represent the exact opposite of what Margaret intended. Instead of a simple story about a young girl learning how to grow into a strong woman with her own identity, who is able to rely on her own wits and succeed, it became for many the one-sided symbol of nostalgia for a particular period in history that existed for a small elite group of slave owners, not at all typical of most Southerners of the time.

When asked her opinion about what made *Gone with the Wind* such a success and her fans so fervent, Margaret opined, "Despite its length and many details, *Gone with the Wind* is basically just a simple yarn of fairly simple people. There's no fine writing; there are no grandiose thoughts; there are no hidden meanings, no symbolism, nothing sensational—nothing, nothing at all that have made other best sellers best-sellers. Then how to explain its appeal from the five-year-old to the ninety-five-year-old? I can't figure it out."

MARGARET MITCHELL *This former flapper set the world (and Atlanta) on fire with the story of Scarlett O'Hara.*

Proof that Margaret Mitchell and her characters continue to be loved can be found in the attendance records of the Margaret Mitchell House and Museum. Founded in 1995, it had 45,000 visitors that year; 55,000 in 1998; and 65,000 in 1999. If you want to add yourself to this number, contact the Official Margaret Mitchell House home page for directions, location, and a calendar of events: **www.gwtw.org**.

Margaret Mitchell, in true fashion of the free-spirited, strong-willed independent archetypal female character she created, went on to endow a medical chair providing full scholarships for African American students that has helped to create some of the best doctors in the United States. By the time she was tragically killed by a speeding taxicab on Peachtree Street in Atlanta at the age of forty-eight, Margaret's greatness, on the basis of one book, was cemented forever in history.

The book lives on. The 1939 movie starring Vivien Leigh and Clark Gable only fueled the flames of fame. And while Mitchell's estate's decision to commission a sequel in the 1990s drew controversy, the resulting book, *Scarlett,* had no dearth of readers. At costume parties, there's always bound to be a Scarlett or two; even Mattel has a Scarlett Barbie. The passion and power of Scarlett and the romance between the two firebrands is eternally appealing.

> *The usual masculine disillusionment is in discovering that a woman has a brain.*
>
> Margaret Mitchell, in *Gone with the Wind.*

§ LAURA INGALLS WILDER *home on the prairie*

On February 7, 1867, Laura Elizabeth Ingalls was born near Pepin, Wisconsin, the site of *Little House in the Big Woods,* the first of her many beloved books. Laura's pioneer family, her parents Charles and Caroline Ingalls, and sisters Mary, Carrie, and Grace, would all be immortalized in Laura's memoirs of her family's travels and adventures. Brother Charles Frederick was never a character in Laura's books, although he was a figure in the television series *Little House on the Prairie,* which was based on the book series.

Women Whose Books
Are Loved Too Much
Adored Authors

The family moved from Wisconsin to Missouri, Kansas, Minnesota, and Iowa, finally settling in De Smet, South Dakota. Each move provided more insight into pioneer life in the growing United States. Seven books—*Little House in the Big Woods* (1932), *Little House on the Prairie* (1935), *On the Banks of Plum Creek* (1937), *By the Shores of Silver Lake* (1939), *The Long Winter* (1940), *Little Town on the Prairie* (1941), and *These Happy Golden Years* (1943)—chronicle Laura's journey from a backwoods Wisconsin girl to a woman ready to create her own happiness in the harsh lands of South Dakota.

The memory of having been read to is a solace one carries through adulthood. It can wash over a multitude of parental sins.

Kathleen Rockwell Lawrence

Wilder would use her life in all of her writing, covering her adulthood, including meeting and marrying Almonzo Wilder, in *Farmer Boy* (1933), *The First Four Years* (1971), *On the Way Home* (1962), and *West from Home* (1974). *On the Way Home,* edited by Laura's only daughter Rose Wilder Lane, and *West from Home,* edited by Roger Lea MacBride, were written after Laura and Almonzo left De Smet and began crisscrossing the United States, finally settling in Mansfield, Missouri, in 1894.

225

But it is young Laura's recollections of her family's adventures that would stand the test of time and attract a following of devoted young fans from all over the world. Laura's books have been translated into forty languages, including Chinese, Dutch, French, German, Italian, Japanese, Spanish, and Swedish.

One fan recounts this story: "My father was in the Army, and moving around was just something my family did. When I was eight, we received moving orders for Germany, and we were to leave halfway through my year in second grade. We had Christmas early so that the presents could be packed with the rest of the household goods and shipped off to our new home. My grandparents, God bless them, gave me the yellow-boxed set of the *Little House on the Prairie* books. I had never read them before, but I was hooked.

"The box held eight books, one for each of my birthdays, and it was heavy. But I would not let the movers take it; I had to read each one right away. I knew I could never wait for the books to arrive with our furniture. I pleaded, begged, and cajoled my parents—and walked onto the long flight to Germany the happiest little girl in the world, waddling onto the plane with the heaviest package I had ever carried. Those books helped me 'pioneer' my way through many moves. How could I complain? Laura never did about moving. She saw the world as a place to grow and expand. She saw moving as an exciting adventure, an exploration into the unknown. I spent the rest of my time as a 'career army brat' looking forward to the next move, and whatever changes would come."

Laura Ingalls Wilder died February 10, 1957, at age ninety, in Mansfield, Missouri, the last surviving member of her pioneering family.

> *Today our way of living and our schools are much different; so many things have made living and learning easier. But the real things haven't changed. It is still best to be honest and truthful, to make the most of what we have; to be happy with simple pleasures and to be cheerful and have courage when things go wrong. Great improvements in living have been made because every American has always been free to pursue his happiness, and so long as Americans are free they will continue to make our country even more wonderful.*

Laura Ingalls Wilder

_____

Though she currently lives in California, Pulitzer Prize-winning author Alice Walker has never forgotten her rural Georgian roots. "You look at old photographs of southern blacks and you see it—a fearlessness, a real determination and proof of a moral center that is absolutely bedrock to the land," she once said. Certainly that strength, particularly in Southern black women, is brilliantly displayed in her most famous novel, *The Color Purple,* which also draws on her memories of the landscape and language of the South.

ALICE WALKER *This Pulitzer Prize-winner is unafraid to speak her own truth and that of her people.*

Walker was born in 1944, the eighth child of poor sharecroppers in Eatonton, Georgia. Her mother encouraged her writing, even going so far as to buy her a typewriter, although she herself made less than $20 a week. In 1967, after college, she married a white man, and the duo lived in Mississippi as the first legally married interracial couple in the state. Her marriage, she claims, had a negative effect on her career because it angered black reviewers who ignored her earlier works, including *In Love and Trouble* and *Meridian.*

It was her third novel, *The Color Purple,* that rocketed her to fame in 1983 (it won both the Pulitzer Prize and the National Book Award) and embroiled her in controversy, particularly with the male African American community, which claimed the work reinforced negative stereotypes about black men. The subsequent movie by Steven Spielberg in 1985 only fanned the flames of the imbroglio. However, women of all races strongly embraced the novel, identifying with Celie, a fourteen-year-old girl who is repeatedly raped by the man she believes to be her father. The children of this union are adopted by a missionary family in Africa. The novel takes the form of letters between Celie and her sister Nettie, who works for the family that has adopted Celie's children.

The literary heir of Zora Neale Hurston and Flannery O'Connor, the prolific "womanist," as she calls herself, has penned novels, short stories, poetry, and essays—seventeen volumes in all so far. Each reveals her deep commitment to social justice, feminism, and, particularly, African American women, as seen through her unique inner vision, a vision she began to develop, she has said, after she became blind in one eye when one of her brothers accidentally shot her with a BB gun. The loss of sight in one eye forced her inward, and she began to carefully observe the people around her. By writing, she has noted, "I'm really paying homage to the people I love, the people who are thought to be dumb and backward but who taught me to see beauty."

She believes strongly in the power of art to help change the world and the artist's responsibility to that power—ideas she expressed in her collection of essays, *In Search of Our Mother's Garden*. In an audiotape entitled *My Life as Myself,* she spoke of her activism: "My way of fighting back is to understand [injustice] and then to create a work that expresses what I understand."

I think there is hope in the South, not in the North.

Alice Walker

§ ANNE RICE *queen of the damned*

What would make a good Irish Catholic girl write about vampires, model her main bloodsucker, Lestat, on a male version of herself, and in her spare time write some of the steamiest sadomasochistic erotica on the market? It might have started as a reaction to being pegged with the name Howard Allen Frances O'Brien by her loving parents, but then again, this was not all that unusual for someone growing up in New Orleans. Before she was ever humiliated on the playground, Anne Rice dumped the Howard Allen and, after a few years of rapid name change experimentation, finally settled on just plain Anne. But since then she's done a fine job of proving there is nothing plain or ordinary about Anne Rice—and there's nothing ordinary about the rabidness of her fans either.

Born in 1941, Anne had the good fortune of being brought up in one of the most uniquely interesting cities in the world, haunted by its charm and mystery. In 1956, when she was just a teenager, her mother died of alcohol abuse. After a brief stay in Texas, where her father relocated, she met poet Stan Rice, whom she married in 1961. From 1964 through 1988, she lived in the San Francisco Bay Area, alternately writing, working odd jobs, soaking up the West Coast's version of quirk and old world charm, and going to school.

In 1972, her daughter Michele (affectionately called "Mouse") died of leukemia. During the seven years that followed, Anne worked on *Interview with a Vampire*—a novel featuring child vampire Claudia, a character based on her deceased daughter. After repeated rejection, the novel was finally published in the mid-1970s to wild acclaim. The mix of horror, blood, sexual tension, and

romantic settings proved a potent, wealth-producing combination, and the prolific Anne has continued to crank out several bestselling series of books dealing with vampires, witches, demons, mummies, and ghosts. Her books have given her the opportunity to revisit her beloved characters and her hometown, again and again. In addition, under the pen names Ann Rampling and A. N. Roquelaure, she has also dabbled in erotica, penning such works as *Exit to Eden* and *Sleeping Beauty*.

Her penchant for having a good time has included a season of book-signings where she wore wedding dresses to all of her appearances, including a special affair in New Orleans where she arrived

ANNE RICE *New Orleans' gothic pride.*

via coffin in an Old Quarter-style jazz funeral procession. But more often than not these shenanigans have resulted in the media's glossing over the deeper, more penetrating and powerful themes found in her work. This distresses her, as she once pointed out in her fan club newsletter, because she uses her "other-worldly characters to delve more deeply into the heart of guilt, love, alienation, bisexuality, loss of grace [and] terror in a meaningless universe."

Her fame is extraordinary. She created quite a stir a few years ago when she criticized the casting of Tom Cruise as Lestat in the movie version of *Interview with a Vampire* (she later recanted). Recently she bought the former St. Elizabeth's Orphanage, a massive old structure that takes up an entire square block in New Orleans, and is in the process of bringing it back to life in a new incarnation as one part home, one part museum, and one part funhouse.

In 1995, she hosted the annual coven party started by her legion of fans from the Vampire Lestat Fan Club at her "orphanage." With a little luck, inspired by our fascination with the unknown and propelled by a multitude of fans worldwide, Anne Rice will continue to turn out her luminous, demon-filled view of the world for years to come.

GETTING HOOKED UP

For Rice lovers, there's a variety of Web sites to browse. The two best are Anne's official site, **www.annerice.com**, and for vampire fans, the Vampire Lestat Fan Club, **www.arvlfc.org/members/webring**.

§ J. K. ROWLING *fairy-tale rise to fame*

The life story of Britain's J. K. Rowling is almost as magical as those she has penned for her bestselling character Harry Potter. Divorced, unemployed, and living on welfare with her baby daughter, she took pen in hand, and Harry Potter popped out—an eleven-year-old boy who discovers he is really a wizard and has a series of marvelous adventures while in wizard school. Although she had written two previous books, the blend of fantasy and suspense she created, along with what Associated Press called "one of the most engaging characters since those Roald Dahl created in *Matilda* and *Charlie and the Chocolate Factory*," spelled instant success. The Harry Potter craze was on, and the former schoolteacher's financial struggles were over.

As of this writing, there are three books: *Harry Potter and the Sorcerer's Stone* (1998), *Harry Potter and the Chamber of Secrets* (1999), and *Harry Potter and the Prisoner of Azkaban* (1999). With each, Rowlings' fame and fortune grows; kids were so eager for the last volume that thousands of American parents were logging onto British bookstore Web sites to have copies airmailed to them when the book was released in England before the U.S. version. (That won't happen again, says the U.S. publisher; from now on it will be simultaneous pub dates around the world.) And there will be more coming—Rowling says that she originally conceived of the story as a seven-book series that would follow Harry until the end of his school days, which is seven years. She plans to publish the last volume in 2003.

The millions of copies being sold in English, French, Greek, Italian, Dutch, Danish, Finnish, Spanish, and Swedish aren't all being read by children. Many adults are fans as well, and book groups are even reading them. Rarely have books that kids love so

233

much also received such critical acclaim—the first volume won the British Book Awards Children's Book of the Year and the Smarties Prize; National Public Radio has featured them, and even the *New York Times* raved, "Harry is destined for greatness."

Women who love books too much

Rowling lived in the English countryside as a girl, wrote her first story when she was six, and attended Exeter University, where she majored in French, worked as a secretary (disastrous, she proclaims), and taught English as a Second Language in Portugal. Her favorite writer of all time, she says, is Jane Austen, but as a child she loved C. S. Lewis' *Narnia* books, as well as *Manxmouse* by Paul Gallico. Such acclaim that she has received rarely comes without a price—her books are considered by some to be promoting paganism, and there has been talk of bans. But if anything, that is merely fueling readers' passions—one Web site has more than 200 postings in support of Harry.

> *I just wrote the sort of thing I liked reading when I was younger (and still enjoy now!). I didn't expect lots of people to like them, in fact, I never really thought much past getting them published.*

J. K. Rowlings, on the success of the *Harry Potter* books

§ REBECCA WELLS *divine inspiration*

In recent publishing history, nothing with the exception of the Harry Potter series has garnered as much enthusiasm and fan devotion as two books about a group of Southern women—*Divine Secrets of the Ya-Ya Sisterhood* and *Little Altars Everywhere*. Inspired

AND DON'T FORGET THESE WRITERS WITH RABID FANS

In no particular order:
Ayn Rand, Jackie Collins, V. C. Andrews, Colleen McCullough, Sheri Tepper, Ursula LeGuin, Erica Jong, Jacqueline Susann, Doris Lessing, Marion Zimmer Bradley, Anaïs Nin.

by the antics of the group of women in the book, thousands of women across the country have formed official Ya-Ya groups to, in the words of author Rebecca Wells on her official Web site, "eat and drink and dance and scream and squeal and above all: PAINT YOUR TOENAILS!!!!!" As of this writing, there are 12,000 postings on the Web site, with bulletin boards that allow Ya-Ya groups to connect with one another, and for neophytes to get initiated. There's even one for teen Ya-Yas.

And what of the woman who started the ruckus? Rebecca Wells is no ordinary Southern belle. While she was raised in central Louisiana, where her family has been since 1795, as a young adult she traveled the country. In Colorado, she studied Buddhism with the Tibetan master Chögyam Rinpoche at the Naropa Institute. A lifelong interest in theater led her to pen, and perform in, a number of very successful plays. Activism in the antinuclear movement took her to the Seattle, where she still lives.

But the novels she's written are firmly rooted in the South. Her first novel, *Little Altars Everywhere,* won the Western States Award when it was first published in 1992. It caught on by word of mouth, fueled by both critical and reader acclaim. But it wasn't until *Divine Secrets of the Ya-Ya Sisterhood* that the Ya-Ya craze was on full steam ahead. Indeed, many readers first read the second novel and then returned to the first. Both books are full of unforgettable characters who know how to have fun and support one another through thick and thin. As Tom Robbins said of *Divine Secrets*, "This is the sweet and sad and goofy monkey-dance of life, as performed by a bevy of unforgettable Southern belles in a verdant garden of moonlit prose. Poignantly coo-coo, the Ya-Yas . . . will prance, priss, ponder, and party their way into your sincere affection."

Women who love books too much

And indeed they have. Readers love Vivi and her daughter Siddalee and Vivi's gaggle of girlfriends who've been friends since childhood and carouse through motherhood, shocking the small community they live in. Fortunately for all of us who want more, Wells is busy on the third book in the series. To join in on the fun, go to **www.ya-ya.com**.

> *I don't know what will happen to Vivi and Sidda in the next Ya-Ya book, any more than I know what my own mother and I will do at lunch tomorrow. . . . My fictional characters . . . have their own rare airwave that, when I'm lucky, I can tune in to.*
>
> Rebecca Wells

AND NOW IT'S YOUR TURN

Who gets your vote as the most important, influential, or just plain favorite Woman Whose Books Are Loved Too Much? See page 275 of this volume to discover how you can nominate *your* worthy women.

appendix
Book Groups: Chatting It Up

Donna Paz

Long before Oprah formed her on-the-air book groups, people gathered in living rooms, libraries, and bookstores to discuss the books they had just read. When the pace of life seems only to increase, the opportunity to take quiet time to savor a book and then to meet with friends and talk about it is a welcome retreat for many; it's no wonder that when Oprah focused on book groups, our whole culture was reminded of the joy and value of reading.

Recently my company sent questionnaires to 1,500 book groups. We discovered that the overwhelming majority of group members are middle-aged, highly educated women in their forties, fifties, and sixties. They're looking for something that they can relate to, but also they're looking for reading that stretches them.

In 1992, our small firm published our first annual book group resource, *Reading Group Choices: Selections for Lively Book Discussions.* Since that first edition, we've met many book group leaders and members. We've enjoyed talking with them about their groups, what they read, and why many have been successful in meeting month after month, some for decades! While most say they participate in a book group for intellectual stimulation, others join to expand their own reading horizons, meet other book lovers, learn from others, or grow personally. Still others want to meet other people, grow spiritually, or discuss cultural and political issues.

Whether you want to meet interesting people or are simply looking for a good excuse to gather regularly with friends, a book group may be the perfect forum for you. While most people find it easy to establish a group and begin gathering, knowing some of the fundamentals of forming and leading a group can help you avoid common pitfalls. Give these items some prior thought to begin your book group on a positive note.

find your focus What is your primary purpose in forming the group? If the focus is social interaction, those who want to plunge right into book discussion will become frustrated. If you want a serious discussion of the classics, those who prefer biographies and popular fiction won't be satisfied. Have some ideas of what you want to get out of the book discussion and the kinds of books you'll choose to read.

by invitation only? Think about who will be in the group. Will the group welcome other members? Is participation by invitation from a current member only? How many people would you like in the discussions?

set some ground rules It's best to be clear from the beginning about the fundamentals of group interaction. Most groups agree that it's valuable to state the ground rules at the first meeting. No cross-talk (talking over someone else), be open to the opinions of others, respectfully disagree, only those who read the book can comment—these all are examples of parameters that help the group function in healthy ways.

logistically thinking Will you serve food? Is there a host for each meeting? Who leads the discussion? Will you rotate leaders for each meeting? How long will your meetings last? Where will you meet, how often, and when?

what to read? Groups generally want books that will affect them personally and that have characters whose actions are discussible. Groups like to compare characters' choices to those they might make themselves. For many groups, developing the discussion topics can be the most challenging; after all, how many of us have loads of extra time to conduct research at the library to provide background on the author, an introduction to the work, and questions for discussion? The good news is that there are a number of resources out there to help.

BOOK GROUP RESOURCES
Forming a Group

The Reading Group Handbook: Everything You Need to Know from Choosing Members to Leading Discussions by Rachel W. Jacobsohn (Hyperion, ISBN 0-7868-8324-3)

Circles of Sisterhood: A Book Discussion Group Guide for Women of Color by Pat Neblett (Writers & Readers, ISBN 0-8631-6245-2)

The Mother-Daughter Book Club: How Ten Busy Mothers and Daughters Came Together to Talk, Laugh and Learn Through Their Love of Reading by Shireen Dodson and Teresa Barker (HarperCollins, ISBN 0-0609-5242-3)

Book Recommendations and Reading Discussion Guides

Reading Group Choices: Selections for Lively Book Discussions (Paz & Associates, 800-260-8605)

Minnesota Women's Press Great Books (Minnesota Women's Press, 612-646-3968)

Reverberations News Journal (Association of Book Group Readers and Leaders, 847-266-0431)

www.readinggroupchoices.com
References all discussion guides known to be currently available from major publishers and independent presses with more than 150 that can be printed directly from the Web site

www.harpercollins.com/readers/index.htm
Guides available from HarperCollins Publishers

www.penguinputnam.com/clubppi/index.htm
Guides available from the Penguin Putnam imprints

www.randomhouse.com/BB/readerscircle/index.html
Guides available from the Random House imprints

www.SimonSays.com/reading/guides
Guides available from Simon and Schuster imprints

For a listing of online book groups, see the Resource Guide that follows.

Donna Paz is the founder of Paz & Associates, a bookstore training and consulting firm. Her firm publishes Reading Group Choices *annually and manages the Web site* **www.readinggroupchoices.com,** *a central online resource for book groups. Donna managed one of the country's leading independent bookstores, is dedicated to fundraising for literacy efforts, and is a past president of the Women's National Book Association. Her favorite tee-shirt reads, "Books, Cats. Life is Good!"*

Resource Guide

BOOKS, MAGAZINES, ORGANIZATIONS

Poets & Writers Magazine
72 Spring Street
New York, NY 10012

BookLovers Magazine
Tracy Walczak, Editor
P. O. Box 511396
Milwaukee, WI 53203-0241
414-384-2300
booklove@execpc.com

The Chronicle Book Club
901 Mission Street
San Francisco, CA 94103

Lavender Salon Reader
Newsletter and Review for Gay
*   and Lesbian Clubs*
Michael L. Nitz, Editor
Lavender Salon Press
$12.00 per year/11 issues
414-738-0497

The Lesbian Review of Books
Loralee MacPike, Editor
P. O. Box 515
Hilo, HI 96721-0515
800-969-9600
email: loralee@hawaii.edu

The Reader's Edge
Mary Caprio, Editor
Paz & Associates
115 Century Oak Drive
Franklin, TN 37069
615-591-9637
www.pazbookbiz.com

The Women's Review of Books
Linda Gardiner, Editor
Wellesley College Center for
    Research on Women
Wellesley, MA 02181
$20.00 per year/11 issues
617-283-2087

Great Books Foundation (GBF)
40 East Huron Street
Chicago, IL 60611
1-800-222-5870

Utne Reader Neighbor Salon
    Association (NSA)
c/o *Utne Reader*
1624 Harmon Place
Minneapolis, MN 55403
$12.00 for lifetime membership
612-338-5040

Café Utne
www.utne.com/café/café.html

BOOKS ON WOMEN AND BOOKS

500 Great Books By Women: A Reader's Guide
Erica Bauemeister, Jesse Larsen, Holly Smith
Penguin USA; 1994; 425 pp.   Resource Guide
ISBN 0-1401-7590-3

Black Women Writing Autobiography: A Tradition within a Tradition
Joanne M. Braxton
Temple University Press; 1989; 242 pp.
ISBN 0-87722-803-5, $18.95
800-447-1656

*The Feminists' Companion to Literature in English: Women Writers
    from the Middle Ages to the Present*
Virginia Blain, Isobel Grundy, Patricia Clements
Yale University Press; 1990; 1,231 pp.
ISBN 0-300-04854-8; $60.00
800-986-7323

*Great Women Writers: The Lives and Works of 135 of the World's
    Most Important Women Writers, from Antiquity to the Present*
Frank N. Magill, ed.
Henry Holt & Company; 1994; 611 pp.; $40.00
800-488-5233

The Norton Book of Women's Lives
Phyllis Rose, ed.
W. W. Norton & Co., Inc.; 1993; 826 pp.
ISBN 0-393-31290-9; $17.95
800-233-44830

Radcliffe Biography Series:Contemporary Portraits of Timeless Women
Addison-Wesley Publishing Co.
Free brochure
800-447-2226

Women who love
books too much *The Way of the Woman Writer*
Janet Lynn Roseman
Haworth Press; 1995; 156 pp.
ISBN 1-56023-860-7; $12.95
800-342-9678

Women of Words
Janet Bukovisnsky, ed., Jenny Powell, illustrator
Running Press; 1994; 176 pp.

The WomenSource Catalog and Review:
    Tools for Connecting the Community of Women
Ilene Rosof, Editor
Ten Speed Press/Celestial Arts; 1995
ISBN 0-89087-768; $22.95
800-841-2665

Women of the Salons
Evelyn Hill
Ayer Company Publishers; 1926; 235 pp.
ISBN 0-8369-1262-4; $19.00
800-282-5413

BOOK GROUPS ONLINE

A&E Book Club: Formed by the cable channel to discuss classic and contemporary fiction: **www.aetv.com/bookclub**

Book Chatter: Monthly club using message boards for discussions: **http://bookchatter.tierranet.com/talk**

The Bookies: Group of people who started discussion about Oprah's picks and then expanded: **www.geocites.com/Athens/Aegean/2515**

Book Lovers: **www.mindmills.net/booklovers**

Canadian Book Clubs: Advice on how to start a club and listing all clubs in Canada including their book lists: **www.canadianbookclubs.com**

Chatelaine: Modern literature discussions sponsored by Canadian magazine *Chatelaine*: **www.chatelaine.com**

The Coffee Will Make You Black Reading Group: Part of the African American Literature Book Club: **www.aalbc.com/discussion/instructions**

discussBooks.com: Features books, book clubs, and discussion groups: **www.discussbooks.com**

On the Shelf: **www.geocities.com/paris/salon/5507**

Oprah's Book Club: Features the star's monthly picks and online discussions: **www.oprah.com**

TheReadersVine.com: Online community of writers and readers: **www.thereadersvine.com**

The Rogue Book Group: Discussions via e-mail. Has smaller groups on topics such as Japanese literature. E-mail: jsadler@polaris.net or at **http://members.tripod.com/~bookgroup/**

SASIALIT Mailing List: Discusses literature of the Indian and South Asia diaspora: **http://is.rice.edu/~riddle/play/sasialit**

The *San Francisco Chronicle* hosts a monthly online discussion of contemporary fiction: **www.sfgate.com/eguide/books/pages/bookclub/**

Western Canon Mailing List: Join a group discussing the great books from Western literature: e-mail pbarnett@geocities.com Women.com Book Club: **women.com/clubs/books.html**

Acknowledgments

I have many to thank for this book, many men and women who share a fierce love of books. My gratitude to:

Vesela Simic and her delightful daughter, Jasmine, whose excellent research and gentle hearts took this book from a prayer to a possibility.

Interns extraordinaire Valerie Bantner and Jill Wright, literati who lit up our days and did great work uncovering the obscure.
Donna Paz for wonderful her piece on book groups, and her unstinting dedication of the "cause of books."

Sharon Donovan, Rosie Levy, Betsy Hollwitz, and Annette Madden, public relations power pack and bright spirits.

Heather McArthur, Jenny Collins, Everton Lopez, and Mignon Freeman, who keep the wheels turning in synch.

Claudia Smelser, Suzanne Albertson, and Ame Beanland, whose keen aesthetics helped inspire the whole project.

Will Glennon, for having infinite patience and vision.

Teresa Coronado, who could probably be cashing in at an Internet start-up, but gifts us with her presence and excellence each and every day.

And, finally, ultimate thanks to my editor, the indefatigable Mary Jane Ryan, who embodies all the finest qualities of a "Woman Who Loves Books Too Much."

Bibliography

Benet's Reader's Encyclopedia, Third Edition. New York: Harper &
    Row, 1987.

Crunden, Robert M. *American Salons.* New York: Oxford University
    Press, 1993.

Dictionary of Literary Biography. Matthew Bruccoli, Editorial
    Director. Detroit, IL: Gale Research Company, 1980.

Fadiman, Clifton, and John S. Major. *The New Lifetime Reading
    Plan.* New York: HarperCollins, 1997.

Gilbert, Sandra M., and Susan Gubar, eds. *The Norton Anthology of
    Literature by Women.* New York: W. W. Norton & Co., 1985.

Goulianos, Joan, ed. *By a Woman Writ.* Baltimore, MD: Penguin
    Books, 1973.

Hardwick, Elizabeth. *Seduction and Betrayal.* New York: Random
    House, 1970.

Hirshfield, Jane, ed. *Women in Praise of the Sacred.* New York: HarperCollins, 1994.

Vicki León. *Uppity Women of Ancient Times.* Berkeley, CA: Conari Press, 1997.

_____. *Uppity Women of Medieval Times.* Berkeley, CA: Conari Press, 1997.

_____. *Uppity Women of the Renaissance.* Berkeley, CA: Conari Press, 1999.

Manguel, Alberto. *A History of Reading.* New York: Penguin Books, 1996.

Merriam-Webster's Encyclopedia of Literature. Springfield, MA: Merriam-Webster, 1995.

Moore, Virginia. *Distinguished Women Writers.* Port Washington, NY: Kennikat Press, Inc., 1962.

Nichols, Joan Kane. *Mary Shelley.* Berkeley, CA: Conari Press, 1998.

Petroski, Henry. *The Book on the Bookshelf.* New York: Alfred Knopf, 1999.

Shockley, Ann Allen. *Afro-American Women Writers, 1746–1933: An Anthology and Critical Guide.* Boston: G. K. Hall & Co., 1988.

Sinott, Susan. *Lorraine Hansberry.* Berkeley, CA: Conari Press, 1999.

Snyder, Jane McIntosh. *The Woman and the Lyre: Women Writers in Classical Greece and Rome.* Carbondale, IL: Southern Illinois University Press, 1989.

Shwartz, Ronald B. *For the Love of Books.* New York: Grosset/Putnam, 1999.

Taylor, Jane H. M., and Lesley Smith, eds. *Women and the Book.* Toronto: The British Library and University of Toronto Press, 1996.

Toth, Susan Allen, and John Coughlan, eds. *Reading Rooms.*New
    York: Doubleday, 1991.

Trager, James. *The Women's Chronology.* New York: Henry Holt,
    1994.

Weiser, Marjorie P. K., and Jean S. Arbiter. *WomanList.* New York:
    Atheneum, 1981.

Index of Names Cited

Women who love
books too much

Index of Works
and Peridodicals Cited

Women who love books too much

Women who love
books too much

General Index